EMBODIED SOCIAL JUSTICE

Embodied Social Justice introduces a body-centered approach to working with oppression, designed for social workers, counselors, educators, and other human service professionals. Grounded in current research, this integrative approach to social justice works directly with the implicit knowledge of our bodies to address imbalances in social power. Consisting of a conceptual framework, case examples, and a model of practice, *Embodied Social Justice* integrates key findings from education, psychology, traumatology, and somatic studies while addressing critical gaps in how these fields have understood and responded to everyday issues of social justice.

Rae Johnson, Ph.D., RSMT, is a queer-identified social worker, somatic movement therapist, and scholar working at the intersection of somatic studies and social justice. They chair the Somatic Studies in Depth Psychology program at Pacifica Graduate Institute in Santa Barbara, California.

EMBODIED SOCIAL JUSTICE

Rae Johnson

Routledge
Taylor & Francis Group

LONDON AND NEW YORK

First published 2018
by Routledge
2 Park Square, Milton Park, Abingdon, Oxon OX14 4RN

and by Routledge
711 Third Avenue, New York, NY 10017

Routledge is an imprint of the Taylor & Francis Group, an informa business

© 2018 Rae Johnson

The right of Rae Johnson to be identified as author of this work has been asserted by them in accordance with sections 77 and 78 of the Copyright, Designs and Patents Act 1988.

British Library Cataloguing-in-Publication Data
A catalogue record for this book is available from the British Library

Library of Cataloging-in-Publication Data
A catalog record for this book has been requested

ISBN: 978-1-138-21768-3 (hbk)
ISBN: 978-1-138-21770-6 (pbk)
ISBN: 978-1-315-43964-8 (ebk)

Typeset in Bembo
by Taylor & Francis Books

Printed and bound by CPI Group (UK) Ltd, Croydon, CR0 4YY

CONTENTS

FIGURES

ACKNOWLEDGEMENTS

I am indebted to the clients, students, and research participants whose stories ground this book in the everyday embodied experience of oppression. I promise to pay it forward.

My dear colleague, Christine Caldwell, has been a source of encouragement and inspired collaboration since the very beginning of this project. I am so fortunate to be able to work with her and call her my friend.

Mary Beattie and Bruce Kidd at the University of Toronto held space for my research when the disciplinary structures of the academy rendered me homeless. Their scholarly integrity is a model for my own teaching.

Kesha Fikes reviewed the draft manuscript with grace, insight, and remarkable generosity. Her feedback strengthened the book in ways I would never have imagined.

And lastly, my gratitude and appreciation to Jill Kern, who listened to my doubts and convictions in equal measure and always encouraged me to find and hold my true North.

Special thanks to the artist Claire Weismann Wilks for the images seen on the book's front and back cover. Claire Weissman Wilks of Toronto, a lithographer, a draughtswoman who worked in monoprints and conte, a sculptor in bronze, clay, and glass, has had one woman shows in galleries and museums in Stockholm, New York, Museo del Chopo (Mexico City), Rome, Jerusalem, Muzejsko galerijski Centar (Croatia) and the major museum in Venice, Querini Stampalia. Her work can be visited on her website: cwwilks.com

1

INTRODUCTION

The lived experience of the body – that is, our bodily sensations, perceptions, and behaviors – is the essential ground of human identity. Developmentally, our visceral impulses serve as the foundation for personal agency, guiding us as we move through the world, reaching for some things and refusing others. Our bodily encounters with the physical environment shape and reshape our understanding of the world; we learn about gravity by falling down and discover how our point of view changes when we walk around and encounter new perspectives. Language, often considered a function of our cognitive capacity for abstraction, is laden with meaningful references to the body that hint at its sensorial roots. Indeed, cognition itself is increasingly understood as deeply intertwined with bodily feeling.[1]

When applied to our understanding of the social world, our embodied experience plays an equally important role. As we navigate interpersonal relationships and learn about the characteristics associated with different groups of people, our bodies help to create and maintain the power dynamics that can arise between us – for instance, by signaling dominance or submission through our gestures and eye contact.[2] We are categorized into sociocultural groups according to physical traits that are marked as desirable or deficient based on their appearance and functioning. Depending on our social identifications, we may learn to treat our bodies as sexual objects or as instruments of labor. In short, our nonverbal communication patterns, beliefs about body norms, and feelings of connection and identification with our bodies are all deeply affected by our assigned membership in different social groups and the privileges associated with that membership.[3]

However, despite the research evidence supporting these ideas, existing models of social justice have not been particularly attentive to the body's role in reproducing oppression[4] in everyday life. Neither have approaches that specialize in working with the felt sense of the body (often grouped into a field called "somatics"[5]) offered many strategies for resolving the tension between the information available to us through bodily explorations of sensation and movement and the data grounded in social power and authority. However, it is possible to address the singular experience of the body in a way that does not bypass the political. Conversely, it is possible to work collectively to transform oppressive social structures while fully recognizing the micro-sociological building blocks that maintain those structures.

An embodied approach to social justice – one that recognizes the degree to which our bodies are implicated in the reproduction of social power – should not be considered a replacement for working on the macro-sociological level to make structural and ideological changes in social institutions such as education or healthcare, or as a substitute for legislative reform. Rather, it works to support change in the relational fabric of our lives so that structural shifts correspond with authentic transformations in attitude, and where legal rights and freedoms are experienced at the core of our beings and manifested in our everyday interactions with others.

A practical example

A brief anecdote may help illustrate these ideas. About twenty years ago, I was facilitating a movement therapy group for survivors of childhood trauma. One of the participants brought an intriguing combination of willingness and reticence to the work of the group; she struggled with group dynamics and finding her voice in group discussions, but there was often a quiet smile on her face and a shy yearning in her eyes. One session we were improvising to music using large chiffon scarves, imagining that our bodies were expressing the qualities of air. As the sound of harp strings floated through the room, I noticed that Toni[6] was moving with more freedom and ease.

When the group sat down together afterwards to discuss our experiences, the grin on her face was impossible not to notice. Beaming with pride, she confided that she had put her arms over her head. I think we were all a little nonplussed by that statement at first, until she explained that her childhood experiences with a physically and emotionally abusive alcoholic father had so stifled her ability to feel free in her own body that she became unable to raise her arms over her head without feeling completely exposed and vulnerable. She had been taught not to take up space, not to reach or strive or rejoice. She had also learned not to expose the vulnerable core of her body to possible physical attack. Although she was now well into her forties, she couldn't remember ever feeling comfortable raising her arms over her head in the presence of others.

It struck me then just how critical the relational dimension of embodiment is, and how the ways we engage with others are so much about the body. From my perspective, there were incredible forces preventing Toni from being in her body, in her own way. That morning, Toni named her father's abuse as one of those forces, but in the course of our continuing work together I heard her name many others – being a street kid, a lesbian, a drug addict, and a psychiatric survivor. On the streets, she learned quickly that being invisible (small movements and hunched posture) meant being less likely to become a target for the random violence of strangers and the unwanted attention of the police. On the locked ward of the psychiatric hospital where she was taken after each suicide attempt, she learned that smiling and nodding led to increased privileges and quicker release. As a young lesbian coming of age in the 1970s, she discovered that there is no room for large, expressive movements in a closet. Street drugs helped to ease the pain by disconnecting her from the scarred and vulnerable body that she had come to hate. Taken together, these life experiences resulted in a tightly restricted movement repertoire overlaid with gestures of passive compliance and a prevailing sense of absence – of not really being present. In the evocative words of Mahershala Ali (2017) in describing the bodily impact of unrelenting persecution, Toni had "folded in" on herself.

In a way, Toni's whole life history of oppression was held in her body – readable in her posture and palpable to others. After that first morning where she risked change by reaching her arms into the air, however, the group dynamic slowly evolved. Toni continued to take more space in the room (physically at first, and then verbally) and she became more expressive (beginning with facial expression and expanding to verbal expression). Eventually, she was able to hold her ground in disagreements with other members of the group. While these transitions were not always smooth, they always contributed to a more engaged, cohesive, and functional group. Over time, Toni and the other group members were able to see their group as a microcosm of the larger world, and to understand their progress within it as also possible outside it.

For Toni, the changes in her nonverbal communication translated to increased agency and presence in her personal and professional life. She harnessed the calm authority of her own bodily sense of right and wrong, stood up to an exploitative landlord, and stubbornly pursued the reinstatement of a lapsed healthcare practitioner's license. She dared to express her attraction to a woman she met at a political rally, and is now happily married. Although Toni's current life is modestly ordinary in many respects – she works two jobs, co-parents three kids, and co-owns a home in a quiet residential neighborhood – it is worlds away from what it was. More importantly, Toni feels different inside herself. She is no longer afraid to breathe, to reach, to be seen, or to push back. These changes show up in how she carries herself, and she conveys them implicitly to those who now look to her for example and inspiration – her children, the students in the healthcare program at the college where she teaches, and the street kids at the inner-city youth center where she volunteers.

Toni's story offers one example of how becoming more attuned to the felt experience of the body can reconnect us to a source of knowledge and strength beyond the social power we are accorded by others. It illustrates how being supported to experiment with bodily expressions of grace and freedom can transform painful and limiting movement patterns. It reveals the social and political dimensions of these patterns, and how behaviors that might otherwise be ascribed to individual weakness are perhaps better understood as an adaptive response to relational threat. Finally, her story suggests how the relational nature of embodiment – that we are always responding to the bodily signals of others and they to ours – can work for social good as well as ill.

In the years since that movement therapy group with Toni, I have continued to develop and refine the insights offered by that single potent gesture of hers. Intrigued by the apparent relationship between trauma, oppression, and the body, I grew more attuned to the possible somatic manifestations of oppression in myself and others, and listened more carefully for connections between what clients told me about their bodies and the social contexts in which they lived.

I also became increasingly interested in how education (both social justice education and somatic education) might bring the embodied dimensions of oppression into a larger conversation. My motives for broadening the discussion beyond the psychotherapeutic context in which I typically worked included my awareness of how social stigma around mental health (not to mention the limited provision of service) restricts psychotherapy's scope of impact. A related tendency (among the public and professionals alike) to pathologize and individualize any issue addressed by psychotherapy was also problematic; I certainly didn't want this discussion framed as something that was "wrong" with "some individuals" who have experienced oppression. Lastly, I hoped that a learning focus, rather than a healing focus, would allow a broader range of practitioners to apply whatever useful knowledge emerged from my research.

Framing the issues

The scholarly work being done in the areas of experiential and anti-oppressive education provided me with important theoretical and practical foundations, especially when integrated with insights and research findings from the fields of nonverbal communication and traumatology. Gradually, the interlocking and intersecting ideas I gathered from many disciplinary areas began to form a rough conceptual framework. While this framework seemed to lend support to my developing theories about the connections between oppression and the body, it also highlighted some gaps in current knowledge, and pointed to some questions that could usefully be asked as part of a formal study.

The conceptual framework outlined below is the result of a strategic review of the literature in educational theory and practice (especially anti-oppressive and somatic education), anthropology (embodiment theories and nonverbal communication research, in particular), and traumatology. Although a more detailed review is provided in subsequent chapters, here I outline some key findings in a sequence that articulates the underlying rationale that anchored my study and from which my research questions eventually emerged.

In short, anti-oppressive educational theories[7] suggest that:

1. we learn oppression through daily lived experience of social and political life; and

2.   it is possible to transform that experience of oppression (and collectively, oppressive social systems) through a process of anti-oppressive education that supports (often through a form of literacy work) the development of a degree of critical consciousness.

Somatic embodiment theories[8] argue that:

1.   we learn through our bodies (not just our minds);
2.   our lived experience is significantly an embodied experience;
3.   our lived experience is necessarily also a social experience; and
4.   it might be possible to transform embodied experience through a process of somatic education that supports (often through a form of somatic literacy) the development of a degree of embodied consciousness.

Research into nonverbal communication[9] proposes that:

1.   we learn about social systems through patterns of interpersonal nonverbal communication;
2.   these patterns of communication can be grouped into categories that assist in recognizing, assessing, and understanding how we communicate (and learn) through our bodies; and
3.   the nonverbal component of social interaction (rather than institutional structure) is the locus for the most common means of social control.

And lastly, research findings in traumatology[10] suggest that:

1.   trauma is mediated through the body and manifested in embodied experience;
2.   oppression is traumatic; and
3.   the effects of trauma can be categorized in ways that assist in recognizing, assessing, and understanding how trauma (and perhaps thereby oppression) impacts embodied experience.

After several years combing through the accumulated knowledge of numerous experts, however, I had still not encountered a comprehensive description of how oppression manifests in and through embodied experience. Nor had I found specific tools, strategies, or approaches for identifying, unpacking, and transforming the somatic impact of oppression. I was left wondering exactly how oppression is experienced in the body, and how we bring our bodies to the navigation of power differentials in our social interactions. I was also curious whether education could resolve some of the negative effects of oppression and provide a means for becoming more conscious and skilled in the way we embody power.

The multi-year study I undertook to help answer these questions represents a preliminary foray into a rich and complex area and offered the beginnings of new knowledge. It introduced embodied experience as both an analytic tool and a means of scholarly inquiry, and started to articulate how people experiencing oppression relate to their bodies and the bodies of others. It also provided insights from their lived experience, suggesting that our embodied knowledge is critically important to our understanding of social justice. After publishing the initial findings of my research, a colleague and I embarked on a second phase of the study that included additional participants, refined the questions being asked, and explored new methodological strategies.

Based on the findings of this research and drawing on two decades of clinical practice with members of marginalized and subordinated social groups, I developed a preliminary model of embodied critical learning designed to address the somatic impact of oppression. I began working with this model with clients and in the graduate courses I taught in counseling psychology, refining it over a period of many years based on my own experience of using the model and on extensive feedback from students and colleagues.

After fielding requests to train people in the model so they could use it in their professional work, I realized there was a need for a more comprehensive document on the subject, beyond the journal articles and research report I had already published. This book represents the culmination of my wide-ranging efforts to better understand how social injustice affects our bodily selves in destructive and painful ways, and how we might unlearn the embodied patterns that keep oppression in place.

Overview of the book

Embodied Social Justice introduces an approach to anti-oppression work designed for use by social workers, counselors, educators, and other human service professionals. The book explores the somatic impact of oppression – that is, how we embody oppressive social conditions through our nonverbal interactions, and how oppression affects our relationship with our own body. In documenting the embodied experiences and understandings of people who identify as oppressed, it offers clear descriptions of how oppression is experienced as a bodily "felt sense" and illuminates the mostly unconscious behaviors that perpetuate inequitable social relations. It then frames this knowledge in an interdisciplinary context, and describes how the embodied knowledge of oppression can contribute to the development of a model of embodied social justice. Consisting of a conceptual framework, case examples, and a model of practice, the book integrates key findings from education, psychology, anthropology, and somatic studies while addressing critical gaps in how these fields have understood and responded to real-life issues of social justice.

Embodied Social Justice is organized into three parts. Part I: Body Stories offers a series of narratives drawn from my research into the embodied experience of oppression. These "body stories" illustrate how racism, sexism, classism, ableism, and heterosexism are experienced in and through the body. The narratives use language that reflects the vivid and visceral qualities of embodied experience and employ direct quotes from participants to provide a real-life context for the model of embodied social justice described in Part III. The final chapter of this section articulates the five themes that emerge from the narrative data, and links the material from the body stories to the research literature in nonverbal communication and traumatology.

The next part (Part II: Oppression and Embodiment) reviews the topic of embodied social justice and some of the scholarly literature in which this book is grounded. It walks the reader through key findings in anti-oppression education and somatic studies and further articulates the problems and gaps in knowledge that served as the conceptual grounding and impetus for my research into the somatic experience of oppression. It also orients the reader to key information that will support their understanding of the model presented in the Part III.

Part III: Grasping and Transforming the Embodied Experience of Oppression introduces a model of transformative learning that privileges body knowledge (e.g., bodily sensation, body image, and nonverbal communication) in exploring issues of social justice. In addition to detailed descriptions of each phase of the cycle, strategies are provided for facilitating and assessing use of the cycle in clinical, educational, and community settings.

The final chapter (Chapter 13: Community Resources) offers suggestions for readers who wish to explore further the topic of embodied social justice, and includes a recommended reading list, links to professional associations and training courses, and websites devoted to the topics of embodiment and social justice.

Notes

1 The assertions in this paragraph are supported by the work of a number scholars across a range of fields. The work of Thomas Csordas (1994) helped me more fully appreciate the fundamental role of the body in experience, and the neuroscience research undertaken by Antonio Damasio (1999) and others undergirds my statement that the body plays a fundamental role in emotion and cognition. I am also indebted to Carrie Noland's work on embodiment and agency (Noland, 2009) and the developmental movement work of Bonnie Bainbridge Cohen (2012).

2 See the nonverbal communication research on issues of social power, in particular Steve Ellyson and John Dovidio's work on power, dominance, and nonverbal behavior (Ellyson and Dovidio, 1985).

3 I understand these aspects of embodied experience as the visceral expressions of social constructions of power and identity, not as manifestations of natural, absolute truths about bodies or selves. Although I believe that we construct the social realities that generate such experiences, my research suggests that we respond to these ideas about the body as if they were real.

4 I define oppression as the unjust use of socially assigned power. Systemically, oppression is often enacted through laws and norms that subjugate members of a subordinated social group to benefit members of the dominant group. According to anti-oppressive educator Kevin Kumashiro (2000, p. 25), "oppression refers to a social dynamic in which certain ways of being in this world – including certain ways of identifying or being identified are normalized or privileged while other ways are disadvantaged or marginalized." Allan Johnson (2001, p. 20) notes that "Oppression is a social phenomenon

that happens between different groups in a society; it is a system of social inequality through which one group is positioned to dominate and benefit from the exploitation and subordination of another." He argues that it is through our implicit values and unconscious behavior that we most effectively collude with a system of oppression, and thereby contribute to its maintenance in a society. Participation in oppressive systems is not optional, but how we participate is. Accepting privilege is a path of least resistance in an oppressive system. According to Johnson, oppression requires no malicious intent, simply a refusal to resist.

5 "Somatics" is a term coined by existential phenomenologist Thomas Hanna, who used it to refer to ways of working with individuals and groups that privilege the first-person subjective experience of the body (Hanna, 1970). It is an umbrella term that encompasses a diverse range of body work, movement approaches, and mind/body practices. A discussion of somatic perspectives and practices is offered in Chapter 10.

6 Toni's real name and identifying details have been changed to protect her privacy.

7 See Chapter 9 for details and sources.

8 See Chapter 10 for details and sources.

9 See Chapter 8 for details and sources.

10 See Chapter 8 for details and sources.

PART I
Body stories

2

EMBODIED INQUIRY

The position of those who carry the burdens of social inequality is a better starting point for understanding the totality of the social world than is the position of those who enjoy its advantages.

(Connell, 1993, p. 39)

As suggested by the epigraph above, understanding how oppressive social systems function (as a necessary precondition of dismantling them) requires a direct understanding of the everyday lives of the oppressed. As I worked to identify and unpack the particular role of the body in oppression, it became increasingly clear to me that any formal or systematic exploration of the topic needed to begin with the stories of those who navigated the embodied dimensions of oppression on a daily basis. From this experiential ground, conceptual frameworks and models of practice might then emerge that could suggest strategies for embodied social change.

Chapter 1 refers to a multi-phase study that a colleague and I conducted into the embodied experience of oppression. Carried out over a ten-year period in multiple locations, this qualitative study employed a methodology that drew on somatic approaches to research, narrative inquiry, and performed ethnography. The first phase of the study[1] involved in-depth semi-structured interviews with twenty individuals who had personal experiences of oppression as well as professional expertise in diversity and equity issues (for example, community activists, anti-oppression educators, and multicultural counselors). We intentionally recruited individuals from a variety of social categories of difference (e.g., race, class, ethnicity, ability, gender identity, age, and sexual orientation) as well as an identified capacity to articulate their somatic experience. In the second phase of the study, a team of researchers[2] crafted the transcribed qualitative data into body-centered narratives that were then performed on stage as interactive, movement-based, spoken-word performance pieces. By communicating the data as performance, we were able to capture the nonverbal nuances of embodied experiences of oppression and incorporate audience response into our understanding of the phenomenon.

In the chapters that follow, I present five of the original body-centered narratives from the study. These narratives, or "body stories," describe the lived embodied experiences and understandings of research participants and are based on their responses to a set of interview questions.[3] In order to help orient the reader to these stories, I first want to highlight some of the uniquely somatic features of the methodology.

For example, believing that a traditional research interview would likely not bring the richness of somatic experience into the process (lots of talking and sitting, not much moving or attending to the body), I decided to expand the data collection strategy to include a few brief somatic exercises. These "experiments" were designed to help elicit certain dimensions of somatic experience that might not be immediately accessible to the participants through verbal questioning alone. These optional experiential components included a guided Focusing® exercise, as well as an interactive boundary exercise to explore issues and patterns in the use of personal space. Both exercises were described to participants before they agreed to participate in the study, and again directly prior to the exercises themselves.

By incorporating interoceptively focused exercises into the interview process, participants were able to access present-moment embodied experience that related to the domains I was curious about. These exercises also served to deepen the engagement between us, as they required the participant to allow me to witness them in spontaneous bodily sensation and in movement interaction. In keeping with Behnke's approach to somatic inquiry (Behnke, 1995), I have included descriptions of the exercises in the end notes of this chapter,[4] in order to provide interested readers with an opportunity to feel in their own body what was discussed and experienced in the interview.

Also, as a somatic researcher, I understand my own body as an instrument of exploration and meaning-making. I attempted to maintain an awareness of this throughout the interviews; that the body of the researcher in relation to the body of the participant shapes the data being shared, with our bodies as both transmitters and receivers of such data. My nonverbal responses (a brief clench of my jaw, an audible sigh, an encouraging smile) were part of the intercorporeal field; my bodily presence affected how participants engaged with the research, including what they said and how they communicated it.

Because of the engaged, embodied, and interactive nature of the interviews, my analysis of the data needed to shift to accommodate the presence of my own body and to recognize the existence of nonverbal information. One of the ways I accomplished this was to take extensive notes to articulate my embodied responses to the interviews and to engage in a process of critical reflexivity, as advocated by Finlay (2005) and Hein (2004). I was also careful to describe (rather than interpret) any nonverbal data.

An embodied approach to data analysis also recognizes that listening to the data with a poet's ear may better illuminate and distill subjective nonverbal material than more literal, mathematical, and/or structured approaches to qualitative data analysis. Chadwick (2012) constructed poems from the transcripts to help her make meaning of women's experiences of childbirth, and I did the same when analyzing the data in this study:

> How do I tell the story of my body?
> How do I bring coherence and transparency
> to random scraps of emotion, sensation, and impulse?
> The wordless knowledge within my cells
> remembers everything, analyzes nothing
> Is it possible to unravel the deeply knotted
> strands of memory and meaning
> that live in the muscles along my spine
> flicker in the synapses at the base of my skull
> linger in the touch receptors long after my brush with reality?
> The stories of my body lie buried in my bones
> waiting for the pull of muscle and sinew
> and the tickle of a deep, deep breath
> to float them to the surface of my skin.

Rather than code the data into small chunks of information (typical in the first stages of qualitative data analysis), I tended to parse out longer phrases and sentences to preserve as much contextual meaning as possible. In keeping with my somatic orientation, I then engaged in a process of embodied reflection[5] on each of these content strings, allowing possible meanings to emerge through a process of implicit embodied knowing. I then looked across all five narratives to create links between them, and to develop overarching themes.

Lastly, in order for the research to be genuinely reflective of a somatic approach, the body must be present in the writing of the research text. Rosemarie Anderson, in her two-part article "Embodied Writing: Presencing the Body in Somatic Research," asserts that traditional scientific and academic writing is "parched of the body's lived experience" (Anderson, 2002a, p. 40). In order to redress this absence, she suggests that research into somatic experience can only be represented through embodied writing, and describes what she considers to be its distinctive features.

1.   First, embodied writing offers vivid depictions of experience intended to invite a somatic response in the reader.
2.   Embodied writing is inclusive of internal and external data but is written from the inside out, letting the soma's "perceptual matrix guide the words, impulse by impulse, sensation by sensation" (Anderson, 2002b, p.43). This does not mean writing that is self-indulgent or meandering; it simply means that the writer needs to be *in their body* when they write.
3.   Embodied writing is descriptive of the rich array of sensory and perceptual material available through somatic experience, and attuned to the deeper

layers of sensual, emotional, and psychological associations, memories, and undercurrents that attend such experience.

4. Lastly, embodied writing privileges the subjective experience of the body over other elements of writing style or content. Although poetic or artistic depictions can often illuminate somatic experience, they are used in the service of lived experience.

Therefore, one of the challenges of creating these body stories was to offer an example of embodied writing that spoke as clearly and deeply as possible without attempting to assert universal truths or establish objective realities about bodies. More importantly, these narratives needed to be more than just clear and accurate; they ought to be evocative. I wanted the reader to have a visceral response to the words on the page, not just an intellectual understanding of their meaning.

With respect to crafting narratives that emerge from experiences of oppression, feminist theorist bell hooks (1994) reminded me to write in a way that promoted the accessibility of anti-oppression theory and research. She argues that because most feminist thinkers and theorists do their work in the elite setting of the university, their work is written in highly academic language that is not easily understood by those outside academe (indeed, it could be argued that some of it is not easily understood within it, either). hooks endorsed, and I have attempted to emulate, a writing style that returns feminism to its grassroots by making its knowledge more broadly accessible.

As a final check of these criteria, a draft of the narrative of each participant's participation was made available for their review and feedback after the first interview, and again prior to the creation of a final draft. In each case, participants noted that their body story not only felt real and authentic to their experience, reading their narrative evoked for them some of the same bodily sensations they experienced during the interview. I hope that readers are able use these body stories as a catalyst for their own embodied reflections on the intersecting nature of power and embodiment.

Notes

1 Institutional Review Board approval was obtained from the home institutions of the principal investigators prior to embarking on the study, and written and/or oral consent was obtained from participants for both phases of the study.

2 My deepest thanks and appreciation to Dr. Christine Caldwell, co-researcher and principal collaborator during the second phase of the study, and to a remarkable research team drawn from graduate students in the Somatic Counseling program at Naropa University: Nora Ahmed-Kamal, Erin Flynn, Chelsea Gregory, Masha Mikulinski, Stefanie Raccuglia, Leah Raulerson, and Cynthia St. Clair.

3 The interviews focused on their personal experiences of oppression, and how these experiences have affected: a) their relationship to their own body and the bodies of others; and b) their nonverbal communication patterns. Although I provided some initial questions for consideration, the process was intended to be an interactive dialogue rather

than a formal question-and-answer interview. Some of the interview questions I asked included the following:

1. What are some of your experiences of oppression?
2. How do you relate those experiences to social categories of oppression (for example, do you understand them as experiences of racism, sexism, or some other form of oppression)?
3. How have your experiences of oppression affected how you relate to your own body? This might include how you view your relationship to your body, how you understand your own body image, or the degree to which you experience a kinesthetic awareness of your body.
4. How have your experiences of oppression affected how you believe others relate to (or read) your body?
5. How have your experiences affected how you relate to (or read) the bodies of others?
6. What role has nonverbal communication – for example, the navigation of personal space, the use of gesture, touch, or eye contact – played in your experiences of oppression? For example, are you aware of modifying your nonverbal communication according to whether or not you feel oppressed in a particular situation? What have you observed in the nonverbal communication of others in these situations?

4 Somatic exercises used in the interviews:

1. Sensing and navigating boundaries:

    a. The research participant and I stood facing one another, about ten feet apart. I began slowly moving toward the participant, while asking them to attend to their inner somatic experience, and to notice when they become aware of signals indicating that their personal boundaries have been reached. At that point, they were to tell me to stop advancing. When I stopped moving forward, participants had the opportunity to ask me to retreat a half step to ensure I was not inside their personal boundary.
    b. After the exercise, we discussed the experience of having me approach them to the limits of their personal space. Some of the questions I asked included: What were the somatic indicators that a boundary had been reached? How was your relationship with space and boundaries related to breath? To eye contact? What were some of the implications of your personal experience of boundaries? To what extent might they be affected by personal or familial traits or attitudes, your experience of oppression, or your response to me as the interviewer?

2. Focusing. Following the six steps of Focusing® as outlined by Eugene Gendlin (1982), I asked participants to focus on and describe the embodied felt experience of oppression. I describe these steps in more detail in Chapter 11.

5 I used Focusing® – an embodied method of accessing and understanding implicit material developed by Eugene Gendlin (1982) – as my primary strategy for distilling meaning from the code strings taken from transcripts.

3

CRISSY'S BODY STORY

Crissy grew up in a small town in northern Ontario of mixed racial and ethnic background; her mother is aboriginal, and her father was white French Canadian. She notes that although her physical appearance does not noticeably mark her as aboriginal, she distinctly recalls the racist teasing she endured in grade school by her young friends and classmates, and the shame that it engendered. For Crissy, racial oppression always seemed to be inextricably intertwined with gender oppression, and the schoolyard taunts often targeted her as both aboriginal and female.

Almost all of the prejudice directed toward Crissy during her early years was also connected in some way to her body. For example, Crissy has vivid memories of being called "squaw" and "longback" by boys at school ("longback" is a derogatory term for aboriginal women designed to draw attention to some aboriginal women's "characteristically" flat buttocks). She recalls how ashamed she used to be of her darker skin; in the summer months, she would get so deeply tanned in the sun that she used to dust baby powder on her arms and legs to make them seem whiter. She also relates the first time she took gym class in a school with a shared girls' shower and change room. The other girls noticed that her nipples were brown, rather than pink like theirs, and made snide comments.

As she grew into adolescence, much of the body shame Crissy experienced focused on her weight. She explains that one of the prevailing prejudices in her community of peers was that aboriginal women tended to be large, and she inferred that having a big stomach was considered a manifestation of her "Native side." When she began to put on some weight, Crissy made the link between body size and her aboriginal heritage, and began to direct her energies to losing weight.

Crissy's attempts to make herself less noticeably aboriginal by staying thin gradually became more desperate, and increasingly dangerous. When she was in ninth grade, she developed bulimia, and began using over-the-counter laxatives as a weight loss method. Eventually, her reliance on them grew to the point that they became a form of currency for her. To illustrate, Crissy tells the story of her interactions with a young woman she babysat for (who was "probably still a teenager herself," Crissy notes). This young woman was sympathetic to Crissy's desire to lose weight, and colluded with her bulimia to the point that she would pay Crissy's babysitting wages in chocolate-flavored laxatives. Her attempts to lose weight evolved into an ongoing battle with her body, as her physical appearance came to represent the primary source of "what was wrong" with her. Over time, Crissy's hatred of her body grew to the point where she would hit herself in the stomach as an expression of her frustration and rage.

Although Crissy eventually realized that her body was becoming dependent on laxatives and began to limit her usage, she notes that the pattern of body hatred and substance abuse that developed during her experience with bulimia was to set the stage for her life as a young adult. When Crissy moved to Toronto at the age of eighteen, she quickly slipped into a lifestyle of drug and alcohol abuse. She notes the continuing connection between drug use and diet, and remembers having conversations with other young women about how effective street drugs were at keeping you thin.

During this time in her life, Crissy also cut her hair very short. In explaining the impulse that motivated this drastic change in her bodily appearance, she notes that in many First Nations cultures hair is considered a manifestation of spirit, and is traditionally left long for that reason. She observes that cutting aboriginal children's hair was common practice by white adults in authority on reserves and in residential schools, in direct disregard for the cultural and spiritual significance of long hair. Crissy then relates a childhood story of how her French-Canadian grandmother used to wait until Crissy's aboriginal mother was out of the house before giving Crissy and her young sister short haircuts. As a young woman in Toronto, however, Crissy describes the impulse to cut her hair as one of wanting to clean herself; she was feeling dirty and ashamed of what she was doing to her body with the drugs and alcohol, and cutting her hair off was both an expression of how powerless she felt, and an attempt at bodily decontamination.

Eventually, Crissy's lifestyle of drug and alcohol use shifted, and she began working at a bank, where she quickly began to rise within the institutional ranks. By the age of twenty-one, she was one of the youngest assistant team leaders at her bank. Despite her success, Crissy continued to experience discrimination and harassment based on her race and gender, and also began to see her relatively young age used as an excuse for patronizing remarks. In one example, she describes how a male colleague would hassle her by repeatedly commenting to others that he and Crissy were going to get married. When she called him on his remarks and warned that she would report his behavior to their supervisor if he didn't stop, her coworker got angry and claimed she "couldn't take a joke." One of her team leaders repeatedly used terms like "pow-wow" and "totem pole" when speaking to Crissy. Others called her "kiddo" and patted her on the head. In each case, any attempt by Crissy to address the behavior was met with anger and denial, and with the insistence that Crissy was overreacting to an innocent remark.

The confusion and frustration that resulted from this denial by others that she was being oppressed has affected Crissy on a very visceral level. When asked to describe the impact of these experiences on her body, Crissy talks about feeling as though her body is being violently shaken by an external force. She feels a "jolt of fear" course through her body, and is unable to focus to see anything. The sensation of being shaken leaves her feeling confused, helpless, and "very emotional." She also feels frozen, as if "stuck between fight and flight." For Crissy, the resulting impulse in these situations of persecution and denial has been to "curl up and endure"; to withdraw on some level while also remaining immobile. As she describes this sensation of being shaken, Crissy comments that this feeling is very familiar to her, as her body reacts to the disruption and disorientation of the assault of oppression.

When it comes to body image, Crissy describes the complex effects of racial oppression as a mixed woman. She talks about having an internal dialogue about her skin color in which she says, "I know that I'm not dark enough," and notes that she often compares her skin color to other Native people. She notes that both aboriginal and white people express surprise when she identifies herself as aboriginal, saying, "Really? You don't look it!"

When she was younger, she admits she had a lot of shame about being part aboriginal. Now she feels proud of her Native roots, but recognizes that her people have gone through a lot despite the current popularity of aboriginal culture and traditions among whites. She cites the commodification of aboriginal ceremonies and the persistent myth of "the noble savage" to acknowledge that some Native people may feel that her claiming of her aboriginal heritage merely takes advantage of recent popular appeal – "Everyone wants to be Indian, right?"

For example, as a student in an Aboriginal Studies program at a large university, Crissy now encounters prejudice based on her skin color that is the complete inverse of the racial discrimination she experienced as a child:

> I was sitting between two white non-Native people in my Indigenous Health class, and one of the very visible Native men in the class was sitting across from me, and he goes, "Hey, I barely recognized you, Crissy, you blend in so well." And then he starts to laugh.

Crissy has also had derogatory comments directed to her in Ojibwe about being "white," on the assumption that she will not understand what they are saying (although she does). What really hurts is when these comments are made by aboriginal people who come from the same geographical area as she does.

Acknowledging the complexity of race and culture with respect to social hierarchies, Crissy describes the power and allure of being able to present herself clearly as simply and completely aboriginal, rather than mixed. She cites an example in a play she has written about her experience of racism, in which she chronicles her experience of coming from a mixed racial background. In it, the main character talks about "dying my hair black and wearing feather earrings" as a way to demonstrate a body image that unambiguously communicates an aboriginal heritage. Later in the play, that character removes her earrings and gives them to an audience member as a way to signal that although this body image may offer clearly readable signals, it does not represent the full truth of her experience.

When asked if there are other areas where she feels oppression and embodiment intersect for her, Crissy talks about her struggle with acne. She teaches movement classes that draw on an ancient cultural tradition emphasizing a holistic approach to human experience and well-being, and finds that having acne complicates her body image as a teacher. For example, she is concerned that her students will assume there is something wrong with her, and that her acne is an outward sign that she is not internally healthy or energetically balanced. When I ask about the relationship between her body image, her acne, and social power, Crissy notes that when she experiences an interpersonal situation in which she feels disempowered, she also often feels an impulse to pick at her pimples. She also talks about the extreme social pressure that she feels as a woman to have clear, beautiful skin – so much so that she is now taking the birth control pill despite the fact that she has strong philosophical and political objections to it. As she tries to find some solutions to the body image problems that the social censure of acne creates, Crissy describes feeling as though she is going against her own beliefs and values just in order to experience some improvement in the appearance of her skin. Despite the fact that acne is not a medically serious condition, Crissy acknowledges that she feels such internalized social pressure to treat it that she is willing to take medication known to put her at risk of blood clots and possible stroke.

As we speak further about the implications of her acne, and the pressure to do something to clear her skin, Crissy describes being caught between the dismay that she is risking harm to her body with the medication she is taking and what she initially describes as her own "vanity." She notes that on some level, she is "willingly buying into" a cultural imperative for women to have clear skin, and then calls herself vain when she attempts to address the problem. As we talk, the double bind that makes gender oppression so effective and easy to perpetuate becomes more visible. Like all women, Crissy is implicitly taught the gender imperative to be beautiful, and then convinced that this imperative is self-generated.

Crissy and I then turn our attention to the ways in which experiences of oppression may have informed how she navigates interpersonal space. When Crissy and I engage in a proxemics personal space boundary exercise together, she is struck by how uncomfortable she feels as I advance toward her. At my first step toward her, she is aware of feeling a bit nervous and fluttery, and her limbs shift involuntarily. As I keep coming, she feels her gut sink a bit. She then laughs involuntarily a few steps before she actually asks me to stop. When I move one step inside the boundary where she had asked me to stop, she is suddenly very much more aware of her face, as though sensation and attention had flooded into that area of her body. I then take one step outside her boundary, and Crissy visibly relaxes.

In discussing this exercise afterwards, Crissy expresses surprise at how threatening it was to have me move toward her so intentionally. She notes that when she laughed, she knew that I had reached her comfort boundary, although she allowed me to advance a few more steps before actually asking me to stop. She notes that when people come really close to her, she becomes uncomfortable that they are looking at her face (specifically her acne), and feels vulnerable and exposed. When I moved one step outside her stated boundary, Crissy observes that she was aware that her body relaxed, and she perceived me as more respectful. When I had invaded her space, she had alternately read my body behavior as threatening. We noted that she experienced the corresponding emotions of being threatened or respected quite strongly, despite the fact that we were engaging in a mutually agreed upon, predetermined exercise in which my actual intentions were neither threatening nor respectful.

Extending this experience into other situations in her life, Crissy talks about experiences in which men have invaded her personal space under the guise of necessity, and where men situated themselves or moved against her in ways that were unnecessarily intimate. She cites an example on a crowded subway car in which a man pressed his pelvis into her buttocks, and another in a supermarket where a male shopper made full body contact as he pushed past her in line. For Crissy, it was clear that neither man needed to be so close, but he used the situation as an opportunity to enact a covert form of sexual assault that could probably never be proven as such.

Crissy also speaks about invasions of her space less related to her body, but connected to a sense of personal territory. For example, her younger sister regularly goes into her bedroom without asking permission (sometimes taking personal belongings), and Crissy finds that this bothers her quite a bit. In a context in which her sister consistently disregards Crissy's privacy and personal space, Crissy questions how the power relationship between them is manifesting in spatial terms, despite the fact that it has been shaped by forces other than oppression. She also speaks about how she uses space in other ways that signal or suggest certain power dynamics. For example, she teaches her movement classes in a circle whenever she can, so that she can be part of the circle, rather than the expert standing at the front.

With respect to body language and gesture, Crissy notes that she is highly sensitive to the nonverbal signals that others give out – whether or not someone smiles or makes eye contact, for example. In talking about some of her childhood experiences of abuse, Crissy relates how she learned to navigate around her mother's anger. She notes that it was the nonverbal expressions of her mother's anger – the angry movements, the look in her eye – that have most affected her.

In terms of how Crissy understands the ways in which her experiences of oppression have influenced her own style of movement, she finds that she has learned how she wants to be in nonverbal relationships with others by knowing what she doesn't want. She notes that she is especially sensitive to issues of invasion. For example, she always asks before she touches the bodies of others. She patted someone on the head once, and still regrets it; she recalls how this was done to her when she was a young woman, and how disempowered and infantilized it made her feel. She also notes that she is very hesitant to touch other people's hair, and very sensitive to having someone touch her own. For instance, she describes how she was at a First Nations event recently and someone behind her reached out and touched her hair, and that she found herself wondering later if they had taken a strand.

Clearly, the relationship between power and the body is very much in evidence in the preceding examples, as it has been throughout my conversations with Crissy. Her narrative elaborates on a number of key ideas with respect to oppression and embodiment. She notes the intersecting dimensions of racism and gender oppression, and how they both worked together to engender a sense of body shame that resulted in addictive and destructive patterns of behavior directed at her body. She vividly describes the embodied traumatic impact of oppression, including the arousal, constriction, and dissociation that result. As she provides compelling accounts of how her body has been the locus of both the wounding and conflict that oppression creates, she also describes how it is the site of potential healing and reclamation.

4

PAT'S BODY STORY

This next body story explores the embodied experiences and insights of a woman named Pat, who describes herself as a "sixty-something lesbian" born and raised in the relative comfort of a white, middle-class family. She has a professional background in body-centered feminist psychotherapy and comes to the interview with me having already explored and transformed many of the somatic effects of oppression she has encountered in her life. Pat's body story is significant to the overall purpose of these stories in several ways; in it, she speaks to issues of the aging body, to the intergenerational transmission of body shame, and to how oppressive power dynamics can surface even in "peer" relationships. Her story also offers an illustration of how somatic psychoeducation can support a person's capacity to articulate the depths and nuances of bodily experience.

When I ask her to describe the ways in which she has experienced oppression, Pat responds by saying:

> I'm thinking that there are three ways that I have known oppression; one is through sexual abuse, one is through being lesbian, and the other is through psychological or interpersonal oppression, as in the use or misuse of personal power and how that gets visited on the marginalized – the dyke, the youngest, or the weakest.

When I inquire whether she understands these three forms of oppression as separate and distinct, Pat goes on to explain that her experience of oppression has been "multifaceted and not compartmentalized. There's a lot of crossover and bleed through."

She also notes that although she has been the victim of the misuse of power along a number of dimensions, the ways in which oppressive interpersonal strategies can affect her has changed, and says:

It's taken me a lot of years of work to develop my own strength, wisdom, and responsibility in an experience of interpersonal oppression. The capacity to recognize it is the first thing. One of the legacies of oppression is the robbing of clear vision. I think that's the worst crime – the robbing of one's own knowing.

In terms of the bodily impact of this inability to know her own experience, Pat then speaks about the inability to inhabit her body fully as one of the core pieces of traumatic fallout. Although she feels that she knows this in more ways than she could possibly recall for the purposes of this conversation, she provides an early example from her elementary school days. When Pat thinks back to physical education class in school, she remembers that she was often made to feel a lack of confidence in her body. She notes that the teachers and coaches were pretty clear in their favoritism of the "natural athletes" and she was never assisted in finding her own capacities, or to develop her own knowing of her body as skillful.

At the same time, Pat acknowledges that she is not inherently unathletic. She now recognizes that she has sufficient capacities within herself to be physically effective in her body. Although she found those capacities later in life – in horse-back riding and archery, for example – her primary sense of her body has always been that she will fail or look foolish. She believes that this early lack of encouragement in school may have stemmed from the fact that physical education teachers "read" in her body a traumatic disconnection caused by earlier experiences of oppression and childhood sexual abuse, which these teachers then "accepted as a kind of truth, rather than facilitated into something else." She speculates that there was a "certain state of collapse" in her body that reflected a similar state of collapse in her psyche. Although she believes that she developed a strong compensatory structure to cope with the impact of childhood abuse, there were limits to her resilience. Under any kind of physical demand or threat, she had no resources available, so that her own reaction of "I can't do this" was accepted as truth.

Pat further notes that a lot of her life she didn't know she was disconnected from herself and her body, but observes in retrospect that there was a strong pattern between her use of various bodily mediated substances and how she was feeling in relationship to herself and others. For example, she notes that she started smoking very early, as a way to stuff her emotions down into the "furthest inaccessible reaches" of her body. She then started drinking alcohol to regain some sense of vitality. The nicotine and alcohol became strategies for modifying her experience of her body in a way that helped her to navigate difficult relationship issues.

As an example, Pat describes a long-term lesbian relationship where her sense of boundaries was persistently distorted, where she was habitually available to being used by her partner – being either elevated or diminished according to their emotional and psychological needs at the time. She explains that if she got too big, she would get slapped down. Other times, she felt as though she was being "shored up" so that she could serve as suitably strong and admirable in order to reflect well on her partner. Pat describes those years as being "*very* not in my body" and notes that although she quit smoking early in this relationship, she immediately took up eating instead. Over the course of the relationship, she gained about forty or fifty pounds.

Pat notes that there was a lot of enmeshment in the relationship, and that even though she believes that she contributed to the blurring of lines of identity, she often experienced a sense of being invaded. For Pat, this relationship reproduced a pattern of boundary transgression and ambiguity established in earlier life experiences. She attributes this to her experience of being sexually abused by her grandfather as a child, and her subsequent inability to set boundaries became interwoven. She explains that because she learned at a young age to tolerate being touched in ways she didn't want to be touched – "to be a good little girl" – she grew up feeling that she didn't have the clarity and capacity to set boundaries with her partner. She consequently used her body weight to create some physical boundaries to compensate for the lack of relational ones. Not surprisingly, their desire for sexual merger was ambivalent, given the pattern of unwanted psychic intrusion. Pat didn't start to lose weight until the relationship was starting to dissolve and she no longer needed the "body armor" to protect herself from invasion by her partner.

After completing that relationship, Pat slowly began to dismantle some of those embodied boundaries. For example, in the course of exploring her body in the context of a subsequent lesbian relationship, she discovered her belly, and then her breath. She learned how much she stores tension in her jaw, and how she holds old patterns of tension in the muscles of her vagina and rectum. Through psychotherapy, her spiritual practice, and increasingly healthy relationships, Pat has gradually retrieved awareness of and connection to her body, and learned how to release some of that tension.

She also feels that she learned how to reconnect with her body through a recent experience of having a Bartholin cyst. To provide some context, she relates that she grew up very close to her older brother. Although he was her "adored older brother," she has concluded in retrospect that he was actually a bully who usually insisted on his own way. When Pat refused to comply with his wishes, he would punish her by cutting off connection with him, employing a tactic of "freezing her out" with emotional inaccessibility. Although no physical or sexual abuse occurred in the context of this relationship, she recalls that his use of power over her felt "very male and gendered" in its nature. For Pat, it was the *energetically* sexual nature of his abuse of power over her as a young child that she connects with the later experience of the Bartholin cyst. Not until the cyst demanded her attention to the point where it required surgery was the memory of the oppressive nature of her relationship with her brother brought to the surface, so that she was able to understand the cyst as a symbolic somatic manifestation of an earlier wounding. The sense of intrusion she experienced during the surgery Pat describes as akin to an "internal psychic rape." She now feels that reclaiming her body through this process of reflection and retrospection is a common pattern for her; that there is always a present-day catalyst that prompts her to uncover how disconnected from her body she has been.

When I ask Pat to talk about how her experiences of oppression have affected her body image, she relates growing up feeling that her body didn't measure up – that it somehow wasn't good enough. Interestingly, she connects these messages back to the same older brother, and to her mother. In the case of her mother, she believes that this sense of inadequacy directly relates to her mother's lack of confidence in her own body appearance. As a young girl, Pat constantly received messages about grooming, dress, and appearance that related only to social expectations, and remembers feeling these injunctions had almost nothing to do with who she really was. Pat's own sense of style and creativity around personal image were imperceptibly but persistently discouraged. As a young woman, she intuitively knew there was something "wrong" with her body in terms of gender presentation. Even before she came to know that she was lesbian, she knew the word "tomboy" and felt that she was caught between impossible demands. She was "never going to be a good enough boy" and she was "never going to be a good enough girl."

Despite this, she learned how to "accentuate my good features" and comply with expectations about how females present their bodies in social situations. Her mother died when Pat was thirty, and Pat began to notice how much her personal style had been influenced by her, but she still dressed to conform to social norms of femininity (high heels and pantyhose, for instance) until she left her last corporate job in her late thirties.

She also explains how the social and familial pressures to appear feminine have affected her masculine side. In retrospect, she now recognizes how much she grieved the loss of her "boy" side that occurred when she began to menstruate. In coming to terms with this loss, and beginning to reclaim her body image for herself, Pat now feels more comfortable to experiment with body image and gender in playful ways. For example, she humorously notes that "sometimes I paint my toenails in the summer, and sometimes I don't." She is also beginning to recognize the ways in which others may be reading her body with respect to sexual identity and erotic energy. When others find her body erotic, it comes as something of a pleasant surprise to Pat, and yet this is now something she can own. Given the work she has done to reclaim her body, she wonders if others are reading not only the external markers of socially sanctioned sexual attractiveness, but are also picking up (and responding to) Pat's increased connection with her own body through subtle nonverbal signals.

In a related way, Pat notes that she has a tendency to feel pressure "not to look" at the bodies of others. She suspects that some of this is related to being lesbian; that she has picked up the heterosexist message that she should not subject others to her gaze as it would make them uncomfortable, and that looking at others might reveal her own sexual orientation in unwelcomed ways. She offers an example of when a bisexual woman with whom she had been having a relationship told Pat that she no longer thought she could have a sexual connection with her. Pat notes that she experienced this rejection almost as an assault. She then felt angry and ashamed that she had let someone in too close. At the same time, she was aware that an erotic energy still existed between the two of them. So, while Pat was feeling disempowered by the shame of being refused (and not just refused, but refused on the grounds of her gender), she was simultaneously empowered by the knowledge that she was still sexually and erotically powerful. Pat recognized that the more powerful she feels, the more she feels a right to look at others. She also notes that when she feels really comfortable about being lesbian, she feels bigger in her body. (As she says this, she takes a deep breath and puts her shoulders back.)

With respect to the overall impact of oppression on her body image, Pat describes the challenges of working through a feeling of internalized shame in which her body is never going to be "okay." For example, Pat went through most of her young adulthood believing that she was overweight, yet a recent review of old photographs revealed that her weight was well within the normal range. Now in her early sixties, she also talks about getting older, and how her body is beginning to change in ways with which she is not entirely comfortable. For example, she is starting to look more like her mother, and despite all the success she has had in reclaiming her body and body image, she notes with regret that there doesn't seem to be any age at which a woman is free of the social pressures to look a certain way. She is aware that she now judges her aging body in yet another critical way, and admires older women who conform to the slim and muscular ideal currently in vogue. Complicating this issue, there are ways in which her body appearance intersects with her felt experience of the body, so that she is aware of feeling better in terms of health and energy when she's slimmer. Given that, Pat's aspiration for the rest of her life is to come to terms with her body, and to feel comfortable in her own skin; not as a far-away ideal, but as an in-the-moment experience.

Pat's experiences of oppression have also influenced the ways in which she uses and reads nonverbal communication, and she notes that she is especially attentive to this dimension of interpersonal interaction. She relates a recent example of sitting with her brother in his backyard and reaching out and touching him on the knee as part of the conversation. She says it felt like a natural extension of their verbal exchange, but says she noticed the gesture particularly because it was one of the first times she didn't feel like a "little sister." She also relates examples of nonverbal communication where power imbalance was very much part of the message. For example, when a waiter repeatedly touched her shoulder during a recent meal at a restaurant, she noticed that she reacted negatively to what she perceived as inappropriately familiar use of touch.

Pat also speaks about how she uses eye contact as a way to regulate degrees of intimacy in relationship to others, and notes that she feels more vulnerable here than in other areas of our discussion. She reveals that making eye contact can be a way to let someone see that she is developing a connection, and that she looks away when the connection feels risky. Avoiding eye contact also becomes a way to limit the degree to which Pat feels "seen" by others. Although she controls access to herself through her gaze, she also acknowledges that sometimes those relational boundaries are set by unnecessary fear, and her nonverbal signals cut her off from something she wants.

In terms of body gesture, Pat notes that she frequently uses her arms and hands to mark the boundaries of interpersonal space between herself and others. She also gestures within the interpersonal space when she's in conversation, and may occasionally reach into the other person's space to touch them. This movement pattern becomes more muted when she is in a situation where she doesn't feel comfortable, and she tends to use more gestures the more empowered she feels. Pat acknowledges that disempowerment has an inhibiting effect on the size and scope of her gestures, and notes that she becomes increasingly self-conscious when she feels that her movements are larger and more expressive than the other person's; that is, when she is not met with some degree of kinesthetic empathy. She also recalls the childhood injunction not to be "too big" or "too much," and how she learned to be gesturally and vocally contained as a crucial part of being "a good little girl." She was taught to "hold it all in" and notes that this inhibition of movement can still emerge in social situations.

Although oppression has clearly had a range of effects on Pat's experience of her body, she insists that merely detailing the impact does not convey what she considers the most important aspect of her experience. On reviewing a draft of our first interview, she found that reading the material was quite a bit harder than talking about it had been, even though she was aware during the interview that she disclosed personal and intimate material. She was aware of an impulse to "massage" and "smooth" her story to make it less stark, but says that she resisted that impulse out of a desire not to dilute the impact of what she'd said. At the same time, however, she is concerned that the impression left by our initial conversation was a portrait of her as a victim of oppression, which she says is an incomplete picture of her full experience.

As an example, Pat cites the physiological and psychological impact of having the Bartholin cyst, and how the journey of coming to terms with both a past and current wounding feels very much like a victory; like an achievement worth celebrating rather than solely a hurt in need of grieving. As Pat speaks further about uncovering the deeper symbolic layers of what the Bartholin cyst represented about her childhood experience and the power imbalance in her relationship with her older brother, she describes her body as the "path to resolution" and a more conscious wisdom and strength around these issues. She describes how she is now able actively to access layers of self and experience that were previously inaccessible to her, and doubts whether she would have been able to reclaim these important elements of her identity had she not experienced what might otherwise have been construed only as a medical "problem." She understands this process as empowering, and takes pains to articulate both the grief and loss that "gets laid down in the body" as well as the "awesomeness of what the body can do with that."

To Pat's way of thinking, it's not that her body was damaged and had to "carry a burden" until it could no longer carry it, so it then became "sick." Rather, she feels that her vagina held some material for her that needed to be held, and the cyst was actually an embodied act of resistance to something relational that needed to be resisted (her brother's gender-based misuse of power in relationship to her). The cyst was her body's way of saying, "Stop right here," and not letting her brother's energy past a certain boundary inside her. Interestingly, when she developed the psychological strength and capacity to look at these issues of oppression, the physical manifestation (i.e., the cyst) moved from being benign to urgent in nature. She was then able to use an experience in which both the physical and emotional dimensions were healed and transformed in a parallel and inextricably intertwined way. She has emerged from this process stronger and more aware, so that she can now identify and refuse similarly oppressive tactics that she encounters in her everyday life. In this way, she is now able to deal with interpersonal misuses of power directly and immediately on a relational level, rather than holding these experiences on a somatic or body level. Facing trauma – whether the current cyst or the buried abuse – shows up the places where fear has constrained her, and where courage makes her expansive. Because Pat recognizes this as a gift, she feels especially passionate about making sure that this aspect of her embodied experiences of oppression is represented as part of her story. In speaking about this, she insists:

> I cannot emphasize enough how important the second part is to the first part of this narrative, because it does not serve me to be a victim of oppression. I do not like that stance, and I have always resisted it.

In describing her grandfather's abuse, she acknowledges that she had initially minimized the scope and seriousness of his behavior, but says that the stance of victim locks her into a polarized dynamic with her abuser as a "big, bad bogey-man" and fails to take into account the profound complexity of human beings. As an example, she speaks about how she has come to realize that although her grandfather was abusive to her, her own father clearly loved him, and for good reasons. She acknowledges the dual truths that her own father received tenderness and gentleness from his father, *and* that what her grandfather did to her was wrong. She sees the lesson of her oppression as a process of learning how to stay in connection with people who misuse her:

> My task is not to make "the other" not abusive. My task is to develop the capacities whereby I am not susceptible to that. I want to go through the painful experiences that my body and psyche put me through in order to develop that kind of capacity … to be a more dispassionate observer.

In so doing, Pat emphasizes how important it is to recognize the fullness of others, not just the way in which those individuals relate to her. From this perspective, she argues that identifying solely as a victim becomes so simplistic as to be completely unworkable as a relational strategy. She further acknowledges a parallel between her own journey toward recognizing the limitations of a polarized conceptualization of social oppression (i.e., there are two separate and mutually exclusive camps: the oppressors and the oppressed). Although she sees the value in exploring those polarities initially as a way to become more conscious of the differences in which human beings are treated and valued, she asserts that we, as a society, need to conceptualize issues of oppression from a much more complex, multi-valenced perspective. In that light, Pat now understands her experiences of oppression as critical to becoming who she is, as they have provided her with a means to encounter, in a very visceral way, one of the more central paradoxes of human interrelationship.

This journey toward a more complex understanding of oppression manifests in her body in a similar way. She has come to understand that rather than resisting when "things go wrong" with her body, she can choose to engage with what is happening in her body, even when what is happening is painful. Being with the embodied effects of oppression has prompted a significant shift in her relationship to her body in distress; she now tries to relate to her body as "always already okay," rather than as something that gets sick and needs to be fixed. "If I've learned to stay connected with my body when it's in pain … and value what's going on even when it's not what I thought I wanted," rather than wonder, "What have I done wrong now?" then she can be with herself with more compassion and less judgement. Additionally, her body becomes a source of wisdom, its symptoms yielding up valuable information to be used, not suppressed.

By extension, Pat notes that if she can increase her capacity to be present with and in her body through a wide range and quality of experience, without disconnection or self-blame, then she can also stay with all kinds of experiences without abandoning herself. This furthers her capacity to be with others even when they are relating to her in ways that are less than ideal for her. In essence, the journey of healing and reclaiming her body has provided a model for being in relationship with others that addresses abuses of power in a way that Pat feels has the potential to provide a larger healing for social oppression. Despite the fact that she has long been passionate about issues of social justice and concepts of body/mind unity, it is her own body's journey that has made these ideas real for her.

Pat's narrative highlights a number of somatic features of oppression, as well as how the body can play a role in resisting and transforming oppressive social interactions. She speaks about how oppression contributed to a disconnection from her body, and how it has affected her body image as well as her use of body language. As she relates her embodied experience as a child abuse survivor and aging lesbian, she makes meaning of those experiences by employing a multifaceted and layered analysis and listening carefully to the messages in her body. She has found that understanding her body in this way has also provided a means of being in relationships with others that feels more balanced and equitable as well as empowering.

5

NATALIE'S BODY STORY

Natalie was raised in a middle-class family in urban Ontario, and identifies as a white, able-bodied, heterosexual female in her mid-thirties. When I ask her to tell me about her experiences of oppression, she begins by describing her early years as essentially happy and unmarked by extreme hardship or limitation. "I think growing up in a white, Anglo-Saxon, Protestant family, I didn't experience much oppression, except for sexism. That's something I'd like to do differently with my own kids." Despite the fact that she didn't feel pressured by her family into becoming traditionally "feminine" in her tastes, activities, and appearance, she does wish that she had "more opportunities to do some of the more masculine activities." She believes that sexism has limited the scope of her life, and feels constricted by the limitations imposed by gender oppression.

Natalie was very aware growing up that she was different from her brother in terms of how her body was supposed to look, and what it was supposed to do. As a girl, she was to wear dresses and skirts, and take dance and figure-skating lessons, while her brother played hockey and soccer. As she reflects on this, Natalie is taken aback by how young she was when she first began to prefer conventionally "feminine" choices for her body in terms of her appearance, movement qualities, and types of physical activity. By the age of six or seven, she remembers envying the frilly, flowery dresses other girls at school wore, and wanting a dress that was just as extravagantly pretty. Although she wasn't aware of it at the time, she observes now that this desire seemed to emerge from her as if it were a natural preference, rather than a reflection of the subtle social gender messages that she had already absorbed.

Her taste in clothing also had direct practical implications for the kinds of activities she engaged in. She cites an everyday example of how the simple act of wearing a dress to school imposed restrictions on whether or not she would play in the schoolyard; the skirt made it hard to move freely, and she was conscious of not wanting to get it dirty. "Looking back, that's sad," she says. Despite an orientation toward a traditionally feminine appearance and comportment, Natalie's curiosity also extended outside these parameters. Once when a childhood girlfriend remarked that she had joined a softball team, Natalie was intrigued by the notion of doing something outside of her usual circle of activities. She raised the possibility of playing softball with her parents, and although she never experienced any direct censure from them (i.e., "Girls don't play softball!"), they failed to support her idea with any enthusiasm, and Natalie never did get involved in the sport. She speculates that because she gave all the outward appearances of being such a "girly-girl," they may have simply assumed that she wouldn't really enjoy playing softball. When I raise this as a possible example of how the ways in which we "read" one another's bodies help to perpetuate stereotypical notions of identity, Natalie agrees completely. She notes that she never felt that her parents were trying to be deliberately sexist; just that they were subject to the same processes and mechanisms of sexism as everyone else.

Natalie credits her relative deficiency in sports ability to this lack of early exposure to more traditionally male pursuits, and wonders if she had been active in sports earlier in life whether she would have built a foundation of body and movement skills that would have allowed her to become more athletic. As an adult, she finds it hard to attempt these activities without the basic sports vocabulary (i.e., throwing, catching, and navigating other players) that many boys develop in childhood. As Natalie reflects further on why she hasn't ever been involved in sports (particularly team sports), she emphasizes that she is willing to acknowledge that perhaps she is just not naturally talented in that area. However, Natalie and I then discuss some of the ways in which there seems to be a gender divide with respect to movement vocabulary.

Natalie cites Iris Young's article "Throwing like a Girl" (Young, 1980), and notes that she never did learn how to throw a ball. She feels that she didn't even know where to start, nor did she feel comfortable about how she might look to others using certain movement qualities (e.g., direct, forceful, or clumsy) that might be viewed as unfeminine. "Guys don't care if they fall when they're reaching for a ball, and I obviously did." She acknowledges that this gender divide with respect to movement vocabulary has two aspects: one related to movement skills, and the other to movement qualities. So not only did Natalie not acquire some of the basic "letters" of the movement alphabet that would have allowed her to form words and phrases that she could have used to play sports, she was also deterred from acquiring those movement skills by a fear of how her body would look if she did.

Although Natalie is very clear not to lay blame in any particular area (she felt no overt discouragement from her parents or teachers, for example), it seems clear that there were no alternate role models who were willing to teach her new ways of being in her body that did not require her to disavow her declared gender identity publicly in some way. In reflecting on the lack of available female role models who were active in sports, Natalie notes that her mother never participated in sports or athletic activities. When Natalie and her siblings were growing up, her father would engage in physical activities with the children, but her mom stood on the sidelines and watched. She couldn't skate, and could barely swim. If she ever joined the kids in the pool, she would "swim elegantly in this little sidestroke, and her hair never got wet." Perhaps unsurprisingly, her mother was also never taught how to play sports.

At the same time, Natalie notes some of the protections against the effects of sexism that her family provided. For example, her father never commented on her physical appearance (either negatively or positively), focusing instead on Natalie's intellectual skills, goals, and accomplishments. She credits her father's emphasis on developing her mental attributes with her subsequent desire to become an academic, and to be judged on the quality of her intellectual achievements rather than exclusively on her appearance. Despite the fact that her family was fairly traditional in terms of her parents' gender roles (her father worked outside the home, and her mother was a homemaker), her father was also an active parent. He "helped out" with many household and parenting responsibilities, and didn't expect her mother to take care of those issues alone.

Natalie's discussion of her family's perspective on parenting and gender roles leads her to note how her upbringing has broadened her perspective beyond the conventions of male privilege. In particular, she observes that her current long-term partner's values may be different from hers due to his more traditionally patriarchal upbringing. In comparing the ways in which her background – and parental expectations – differ from his, Natalie also notes that issues of culture, ethnicity, and race figure very significantly in her relationship with her partner. She and her partner have talked a lot about his experience of racism as an Indian living in Canada, and she observes that her own experience of growing up white in a predominantly white area allowed her the luxury of not having to deal with the issue of race until her family moved to Trinidad when she was twelve. She describes this as the first time she was aware of racism. For example, despite the fact that Trinidad's population is predominantly black, the largely white school that Natalie attended was by far the most prestigious in the country. She remembers walking downtown and having black people call her "whitey." These childhood experiences, combined with her more recent experiences of living in multicultural Toronto and learning about her partner's experiences of racism, have raised the issue of race for her so that she now considers it the most significant form of social oppression.

Natalie notes that her understanding of racism has also been informed by the fact that her Indian partner's parents have not been supportive of their relationship, and have not recognized her or included her in their family. Over the course of their relationship, Natalie has come to question the motivations behind her partner's parents' censure of her, and wonders if it might be not only a case of wanting to preserve their own cultural heritage by excluding someone who is a member of a dominant culture, but also an example of prejudice. She notes that although she has actively taken on learning as much as she can about Indian culture and practice (for example, she fasts on Mondays along with her partner, in observation of Hindu custom), this has not seemed to affect his parents' disregard for her.

Natalie frames the experience of being excluded from her partner's culture because she is white as having a significant impact on her experience of embodiment as an adult. She describes being at Indian cultural gatherings and feeling deeply out of place due to the color of her skin. In the early stages of their relationship, the friction and discomfort that "being white" caused within her was so strong that she often found herself fervently wishing that she was brown-skinned instead. Over time, Natalie's feelings about her own racial background have evolved, so that she no longer wishes she weren't white. At first, she was angry that her partner's parents' obvious dislike of her seems to be based solely on her skin color (after seven years, they still refuse to meet her because she is white). Next, she began to realize that she (not just her partner) has a cultural heritage that is worth preserving. This has shifted her perspective on race and ethnicity toward a more complex and nuanced understanding of these issues.

When examining the impact of these experiences in relation to her body, Natalie describes an initial sense of disconnection from her body in relation to experiences of gender and racial bias. Although she notes the stress of feeling as though her body is wrong in some way, Natalie acknowledges that she grew up not paying much attention to her body, and affirms that to some extent this might have been afforded by a degree of privilege around oppression and embodiment. Because she was white and able-bodied, for example, she had the luxury of not dealing with the embodied effects of those forms of oppression.

At the same time, she recognizes the lack of freedom in her body brought about by the restrictions imposed by social expectations around gender. Natalie observes that the sense of restriction imposed by gender oppression that she described as a child has continued into her adult life, despite the fact that – like many forms of oppression – its pervasiveness often makes it nearly impossible to identify. Natalie notes the impact of sexism on how she experiences other people looking at her body, resulting in the development of a finely attuned sensitivity to the gaze of others:

> I would be very surprised that any female walking down the street wouldn't be conscious of … people watching you, of men watching you in particular, and how you have to be a little bit more … conscious of that … conscious of what you're wearing, conscious of space, those sorts of things … what side of the street I walk down if a group of men are having lunch on the side of the street. Maybe it's not a horribly damaging thing, but it's something that has oppressed me throughout my life. I hadn't been able to name it before I started doing research (into embodiment) but that has had the most impact on me … the frustration of just walking down the street and being aware of men looking at you in a way that doesn't feel comfortable.

Natalie also hates it when men she doesn't know tell her to smile (demonstrating how gender privilege extends to dictating the bodily expressions of others), and insists, "Space is another huge thing." She can recall numberless occasions riding the bus or subway where men sprawl over the seats to take up as much space as they want, even when that spills over into her space. As an example, Natalie talks about sitting on the bus recently when her leg muscles started to go into spasm. She then realized that because the man sitting next to her was crowding into her seat, she had constricted herself so tightly that her legs had begun to cramp. She had literally embodied the gendered message that women shouldn't take up much space, and her body had paid the price in tension and pain. She observes:

> Because it's so subtle, because it's something that you're not really conscious of … it can have an even more devastating effect on your life. It's hard to know what the answer is to that, too, because I don't feel comfortable … shifting over onto his side.

It is worth noting that although Natalie is now able to recognize how retreating in the face of an invasion of her personal space hurts her body, she does not yet have another way of sitting on the bus.

She then speaks briefly about the intersection between gender oppression, her body, and the larger spatial environment (as opposed to the navigation of inter-personal space). In particular, she mourns the loss of engagement with the natural environment through her body – being able to run in the woods, or explore a field. She notes that this restriction has continued from childhood into adulthood, and that concerns about her physical safety still dictate where and when she goes running, and limits the ways in which she is able to engage with her body. Natalie has also noticed the effects of sexism and classism on her body image, and how she presents herself. She notes, "If I put on my tight jeans and my heels … I'm going to get a different reaction than if I go out in my sweatpants." At the same time, she acknowledges that she likes it when people comment positively on her appearance, and enjoys being able to access class privilege when she dresses a certain way, citing the example of getting better service in stores when she has dressed up.

In terms of body image with respect to weight, fat oppression has had a strong impact on Natalie, despite the fact that she has always been slim. Even as a young child, she understood how much cultural capital being thin afforded her, both in her mother's eyes and in the eyes of others. She notes that this positive regard in relation to her weight increased as she entered adolescence:

> I remember my older sister having her cool friends from high school coming over when I was in Grade 7 and saying, "Oh, look how skinny she is, that's so nice," and I remember thinking this is important … realizing that this [thin-ness] is something I need to maintain.

Although Natalie's body was naturally slender, her mother and younger sister both struggled with their weight. Her mother was constantly putting pressure on Natalie's sister to lose weight in an attempt to protect her from the negative consequences of being fat in a society that reveres thinness. Ironically,

Natalie now realizes that this pressure reinforced fat-phobic attitudes, and caused her to view her own thinness as something that must be preserved at all costs and was a critically valuable aspect of her identity, regardless of the fact that she had done nothing to acquire, cultivate, or deserve it. Despite her own thinness, fat oppression became a mechanism by which Natalie was encouraged to view her body as an object whose appearance must conform to external expectations and desires.

When I ask Natalie to reflect on an overarching metaphor that speaks to her experiences of oppression and embodiment, she offers the image of a cocoon. This image contains within it the soft gauzy layers of protection and unawareness that her privilege provided, and the sense of containment and limitation imposed by gender oppression. It also suggests a process of transformation and emergence, although one still in the beginning stages. Natalie acknowledges that the first step in the process for her has been awareness, and that awareness is not always followed immediately by the capacity for change. For example, when she thinks about how long it took for her to notice how her sense of her body had been shaped by oppression, she notes:

> It took me this long to realize what that was. As a parent, how on earth can I possibly make this any different [for my children]? Because it's not just my parents. And just wanting this to be different. As much as it's good to realize, there's also this sense of hopelessness, because how can I make this different? I don't know if this is just a fact of where I am now, because I feel this is a process. A few years ago I didn't even have awareness. Now I'm gaining awareness about oppression and embodiment and all those things, but I'm not sure what the action should be yet. I don't think that's a bad thing, but there is this sense of hopelessness in general … I'm at this place where I feel kind of lost. I think it's just part of the process … but this is where I'm at.

At the same time, it's clear that Natalie has taken some definite steps in addressing the somatic effects of oppression, including becoming more in touch with her bodily experience. The process of reconnecting with her body has significantly involved her academic work with a faculty member who is researching issues of embodiment. Natalie also believes that she has become more accepting of her body as she grows older. She notes that becoming more involved with athletics (especially running) and yoga has also helped her to feel more connected with her body:

> One of the things we talk about in yoga a lot is just accepting your body for where it's at. For example, I am not a flexible person. I'm not very good at yoga. But my instructor is fabulous. She makes you feel like you're doing what you should be for your body right now. Yoga's really helped me feel more in tune with my body, to listen to my body. Until then, so often students just deny their body and that's seen as a positive thing … deny your

body sleep, or good nutrition, or exercise. You're almost told that that's a good thing, that you should be commended for all those things. I think the practice of yoga, of listening to your body … made me like my body more.

Lastly, Natalie has found that her father's death (which occurred around the same time as she moved to Toronto, started her Master's degree, and began yoga) served as a wake-up call for her with respect to caring for her body. She describes the process of watching her father's body decline rapidly before he died; how it was both "horrifying" to see, and an inspiration to the endurance of the human body when it is aligned with a will to survive. At the same time, she feels she has now become more sensitized to the negative consequences of ignoring the needs of the body, by noticing how often her father put his own bodily needs behind the demands of work and family life. As a result, she has become more attuned to pacing her life so that she can live in a way that honors the needs and limits of her body.

Although Natalie may not yet feel she has the knowledge and skill to address fully all the ways in which her body has been constrained, denied, or disconnected as a result of oppression, she articulates a number of key issues, and demonstrates a commitment to personal and social change on a body level. She describes herself as living far more "in her body" and "from her body" than ever before, and speaks compellingly of her desire to translate those changes into the next generation, so that her children will have an embodied example of resistance to oppression in ways she herself did not.

Natalie's body story offers a number of insights into the bodily impact of social norms, privilege, and bias. As a woman, she describes the constriction and limitation of gender performance norms on her movement vocabulary, and mourns the loss of engagement and skill that she might otherwise have developed. She observes the intergenerational nature of the particular manifestation of gender oppression, and notes that her mother also played a significant role in defining ideal body image with respect to weight. Natalie's story also clearly reflects how gender oppression has tuned her sensitivity and response to body language, especially with the respect to the use of interpersonal space.

6

ZAYLIE'S BODY STORY

Zaylie explains that she has experienced a number of forms of oppression throughout her life, including sexism, racism, and classism. She grew up in a white, working-class neighborhood in a small, predominantly white Canadian city, and recalls a pervasive sense of racism growing up. She and her brother were often called names, and her mother (who is black) was frequently subjected to verbal abuse and other forms of racist harassment. Growing up, she felt that other people made assumptions about what she was like, and what kinds of things she was going to do with her life based on her skin color. Zaylie describes her father (who is white) as "pretty sexist," and notes that her mother's internalized oppression often led her to criticize her children's behavior in racialized terms, urging Zaylie and her brother not to "act so ghetto."

Zaylie moved away from home at a young age, in part to escape the oppression and discrimination she faced in the white, working-class world in which she grew up. However, she finds that she continues to be marginalized or mistreated due to other people's assumptions about her based on her gender, race, and class background. Although she describes herself as now moving in a number of intersecting "worlds," each social environment discriminates against her, albeit in slightly differing ways.

For example, although Zaylie is involved in "social activism" circles in the city where she lives, she still finds them white-dominated, despite the fact that there is often more acknowledgement of gender issues, and inclusion of feminist perspectives. Even in an environment where social justice is a central concern, Zaylie describes the discrimination she experiences as merely "subtler" or taking the form of a "tokenizing kind of oppression based on race and class." In reflecting on her first experiences with social justice communities, she sees now how much gender, race, and class privilege was pervasive yet invisible to her at the time. "I tried to fight for my power where I could, and let myself be exoticized just to get listened to."

As a professional dancer, Zaylie finds that she is frequently regarded as exotic or anomalous in the "legitimate art" worlds of dance and theatre. For example, she may be excluded from dancing a particular role because she's black. At the same time, the subculture of professional dance often treats all dancers in a troupe or company with a remarkable uniformity, as if their bodies were interchangeable. Zaylie struggles to blend in, while simultaneously recognizing that she is usually the only non-white woman on stage. Most often, her response to the alienation she feels in these situations is to stay silent and try even harder to be better than the other dancers, to prove that she deserves to belong. She describes these artistic circles as strangely apolitical spaces where issues of oppression or social inequity fail to be addressed in any direct or substantive way.

These undercurrents of oppression based on race and class manifest differently in one of the other "worlds" of dance that Zaylie inhabits. She describes herself as having been a stripper for "a long time," and notes that in this world her skin color can be an asset in terms suggesting a connection between exoticism and eroticism. Perceptions about her race change based on location, however. In California, for example, she is not seen as black – at least not by people who might hire her to dance or pose for photographs. In Canada, she is. She notices this shows up particularly in the kind of assumptions her strip club employers and co-workers make about her: why she's there; what the rest of her life is like; and whether or not she should be given the benefit of the doubt in cases of interpersonal conflict or misunderstanding. In both dance worlds, however, she finds she is more often than not treated as "just a body" that is tolerated provided she does her job and "doesn't leave any residue anywhere."

The third world of dance Zaylie inhabits is the hip-hop community. Although discrimination based on race is not a factor for her here, she describes this community as oppressive in other ways:

> I feel like there's a phenomenal amount of sexism happening there, and gender violence and sexual violence. I've been raped twice by guys from that community, and it's been hard to deal with. It can be pretty out of hand. But it's a culture that I strongly identify with, too, so it's important for me to stay there.

Zaylie also works as a physiotherapist in a large healthcare organization, and she is a student at the University of Toronto. In the world of healthcare, she is a member of what is considered the "professional staff" (e.g., doctors, nurses, therapists), who are almost exclusively white. In contrast, the "support staff" (e.g., caretakers, healthcare aides) are often black, from the Caribbean, or Asian, from the Philippines. In her workplace, she is the only professional who is not white or East Asian. The racial discrimination she experiences there manifests in very concrete ways; for example, she is classified differently from other physiotherapy staff and denied benefits other staff members receive. In a perhaps somewhat more benign but equally telling example of the kind of assumptions white people in Canada make about black people, she is still often asked if she is getting used to the cold weather, despite the fact that she was born and raised in Winnipeg, which boasts average winter temperatures that are well below freezing.

Zaylie also notes a difference in class background from most of the other professional staff:

> If you're not the norm, you just try to hide it, or not talk about it as much as you possibly can. You try to join in conversations where (professional) people are talking about their fucking parents' yacht, or whatever, and you just try to fit in. You try not to point out, "Oh my God, what's wrong with you people?" There are also working-class white people among the support staff, and I feel a certain amount of kinship with them, and will talk with them, whereas the professional staff will look down on them, and say, "Oh my God, they're all lazy."

Understandably, trying to balance between the intersecting race/class fault lines within the hospital staff creates tension for Zaylie. Most of the time she feels that she is "not respected by the professional staff" and wants to get out. At the same time, she feels that it is important for her to stay for the benefit of patients who would not otherwise have access to a professional who might understand their health concerns as they relate to issues of race, ethnicity, or culture.

As a university student, Zaylie finds the biggest problem she has in terms of oppressive attitudes is when people treat her as though she doesn't belong, and assume that they are smarter than she is. She finds that members of the academic community often pretend they don't understand her. For example, when she speaks in class, fellow students often dismiss what she's saying as incomprehensible, simply because she's not using the kind of language that signals the class and race privilege they consider a hallmark of academic discourse. At the same time, Zaylie notes that her program is "pretty mixed"; many students work, or are back in school after an extended absence, and there are varying degrees of privilege among them. Despite the kind of diversity that could engender openness to difference and support for a range of student experience, Zaylie has found it hard to meet some one in the program who really cares how she's doing. "Everyone's very self-serving, and thinks they're the greatest … they're very absorbed in what they're doing."

Lastly, Zaylie talks about the oppression she has experienced in the context of her primary relationship. She has been in a non-monogamous relationship with a man for the last six years, and although they have both been involved with other men and women over that time period, they have been consistently together in some way. She finds that "his family can be really racist." Looking back, Zaylie acknowledges that racism has been an element of most of her other dating relationships as well; it's just that she didn't think about it much at the time.

This retrospective recognition of oppression also holds true for Zaylie's experience of her mother when she was growing up. She remembers that she would often wonder why her mother seemed to be so reactive to issues of race when Zaylie didn't necessarily see it:

> We'd be like, "You're so paranoid, what's your problem?" when she would think that the neighbors were talking about her or laughing at her … and now I feel, like, sure they were. And even if they weren't … how did my father or my brother and I dare deny her experience? How could we say she was crazy?

The impact of all of these experiences of social oppression on her body has been understandably profound. Much of the impact intersects with the uniquely oppressive subcultures of dance, given her extensive involvement with a range of dance forms. For example, the world of professional dance has emerged from a white, Eurocentric tradition that can still be best exemplified by an aesthetic promoted by choreographers and artistic directors like George Balanchine,[1] who wanted dancers who were uniformly pale, tall, and thin (Kristy, 1996). For Zaylie, inclusion in this world has meant conforming to its aesthetic through a strange equation in which being thinner becomes a route toward being whiter. She strives to be as thin as possible as a way to minimize the differences between her and white dancers, and increase her share of the cultural capital afforded by being thin.

Another feature of this world emerges from its perspective on embodiment as translated through its pedagogy. In ballet, tap, jazz, and modern dance classes around the world, technique is usually taught by observing your body in the large floor-to-ceiling mirrors that are installed in every dance studio. Students are taught to view their body movements with a detached, objective analysis, correcting errors in technique by seeing them in the mirror and adjusting their bodies until their images conform to the ideal promoted by the teacher. Even though students must also learn how to "feel" when their bodies are out of proper alignment without the use of a mirror, the perspective of detached, unfeeling observer is retained. How you *look* always takes precedence over how you *feel*, as dancers learn to dance through pain in much the same way as professional sports players learn to "play hurt."

For Zaylie, the perspective on her body taught through these methods (she refers to them collectively as "white dance") was one of disembodiment. In contrast, she finds black dance forms (such as hip-hop or traditional African and Caribbean dance) much more embodied, as the objective is not so much to look a certain way, but to communicate a particular feeling in the body. Through her training in both approaches, Zaylie has developed an extensive movement vocabulary that she has learned to use as a resource in resisting oppression, even as the subcultures of some dance forms are inherently oppressive.

When I ask how this translates to her daily lived experience, Zaylie offers a number of examples. She consciously uses her learned capacity to articulate concise nonverbal messages as a way to resist or deflect oppression. For instance, when she's feeling marginalized during a hospital staff meeting, she may sit a little taller in her seat and hold her head a certain way to communicate an array of messages: that she belongs there and feels entitled to contribute to the conversation; that she is unhappy with the way the conversation is going; that she is strong and intelligent; or that she is prepared to regard others in a critical light. She also uses physical contact to get others to pay attention when she feels they have been ignoring her.

Conversely, Zaylie will withdraw physical contact and expand her kinesphere[2] in response to feeling judged. Although she prefers to engage with others using relatively close interpersonal space boundaries (she describes this as her natural style, affirmed in the boundaries exercise we did together), she will move back and deliberately mute her gestures as a way to withhold part of herself from others she feels might abuse her. She understands her body language to be such an essential part of her that refusing to be physically expressive in the presence of others is akin to denying them access to her.

In much the same way, Zaylie is disturbed by certain movement behaviors of others who may try to use their power against her. She notes that she hates it when men stand behind her, and when I ask why, she says it's because she cannot see their bodies. This particular configuration of bodies and space means that a man can look at her and read her movements, while she is unable to do the same. Because she relies so much on reading the bodies of others to predict who is safe to be with, and because men have so much more physical and social power than she does as a woman, she is uncomfortable being so close to them without being able to read their body language.

The somatic boundary exercise Zaylie and I engage in as part of the interview process generates of further insight about Zaylie's use and understanding of personal space in relation to others. Initially, she notes that she is not very close to many people in her life, and remarks how pleasant it is to be close enough to someone else that you can feel their body heat. When I take a step away from her as a structured part of the exercise, she describes feeling a little bit of disappointment; she wonders if perhaps I didn't want to be that close to her. Zaylie also acknowledges a further dimension to close physical proximity, noting that "sometimes when someone gets close to me, it's because they expect sexual intimacy."

The Focusing® exercise elicits strong imagery in response to my query about how oppression has affected her body. Quickly and easily slipping into focus as she attended to her embodied knowing, Zaylie notes a number of sensations and images:

> When you first asked me … what came to me was that my body is hungry and dry and parched. Then the more I thought about it, I started to feel uncomfortable … that there was this kind of tar coating all of my insides that was stopping me from absorbing anything. Like everything that would come into me would just pass through.

Zaylie describes this tarry substance as something she ingested from the outside world, and that now exists within her body as the residue of her experiences of oppression. She further acknowledges that this residue prevents her from absorbing emotional, psychological, and relational nutrients – from being affected by positive experiences with others. It is not just that her body lives with the residual effects of oppression, but that oppression interferes with her capacity to engage with and be nourished by the world.

Notwithstanding the damage that oppression has enacted on her body, Zaylie also uses her body to generate feelings of power, both publicly and privately. Ironically, she cites the movement vocabulary of exotic/erotic dancing as being able to engender and communicate these experiences. Despite the stereotype of sex workers as hopelessly entangled in their own oppression, and the environment of a strip club as one in which dancers display their bodies for the gratification of others, strippers also hold a form of power over their audience. Zaylie talks about the sexual desire she elicits through her dancing as a potent drug that she delivers through her body movements, and the men who watch her as addicts. The fact that she can give them something they need (and perhaps cannot get anywhere else) means that Zaylie's body is a source of power despite the obvious fact of gender oppression.

The truth of this may be best exemplified by Zaylie's initial response to my question of how she resists oppression through her body. After a moment's pause, she tells me that sometimes when she's feeling really trashed by the world, she goes home and puts on some music. Then she performs her own striptease in front of a mirror. Watching herself in the mirror provides a safe but intimate viewpoint from which to witness her own capacity to seduce and captivate the attention of others. At the same time, it affirms her as worthy of the kind of attention she is giving herself. If erotic dancing is a form of bodily expression with respect to sexual power (however shaped by gender oppression), then it makes sense that dancing for herself returns to Zaylie some of the power her body is capable of creating.

Zaylie's narrative underscores the degree to which oppression functions in subtle and not-so-subtle ways across a number of social circles, and how the degree to which various forms of oppression operate in a particular setting shifts according to context. It also illustrates how multiple forms of oppression work together; for example, how sexism and racism intersect to make being "thinner a route toward being whiter." Zaylie's body story offers compelling examples of education as teaching oppression; for instance, how somatic dissociation is explicitly taught in "white" dance. Ironically, dance education also provided the movement vocabulary Zaylie has learned to use as a resource in resisting oppression, including a highly tuned sensitivity to the body language of others, and the capacity to use her own body to generate feelings of power.

Notes

1 George Balanchine (1904–1983) was the founding artistic director of the New York City Ballet, and is often cited as the single most influential figure in contemporary American ballet.
2 A kinesphere is a concept developed by movement analyst Rudolph Laban that describes an imaginary bubble of space extending around a person in which their movements occur.

7

RAE'S BODY STORY

With some caution, I have decided to include my own narrative as part of this book, despite the fact that I cannot afford myself the same protection of anonymity as the other research participants. The most significant factor in this decision represents an extension of the professional ethics I consider fundamental to my practice. Simply stated, this ethic translates to, "Don't ask someone else (client, student, research participant) to do something you yourself have not done, or would be unwilling to do." Writing my own body story provided me with an experiential ground from which to appreciate the courage and risk my research participants took in telling me their stories, and guided me in the process of trying to do justice to their efforts. Writing my own narrative also allowed me to include aspects of embodied experience that were not necessarily addressed in the other narratives, and to feel freer to suggest interpretations about those experiences, without the risk of "leading" a participant to connections they would not otherwise have made. Lastly, including my own story positions me within this research in a way that no other action could achieve – it requires me to stand behind a process that I am proposing as an act of political resistance through reclaiming embodied knowledge.

Through this process, I have learned (and am still learning) how revealing myself to other people makes me more available to myself; how the conscious creation of my own narrative in relation to the larger human story weaves together aspects of myself that had been forgotten or abandoned, and connects them to the world. The stories I will relate here are instruments of that project. Their purpose is to help me become more fully and consciously who I am, to practice getting at myself through my visceral, embodied senses.

To that end, I have two stories to tell. The first, and most central to my intentions here, is the story of my body as shadow, as the abjected other in the larger story of my life. It is the story of how I came to dislike, fear, and mistrust my body as an inferior aspect of my identity. In the spirit of Thomas Edison, who insisted that "the chief function of the body is to carry the brain around," I came to disown the corporeal reality of my body in favor of attending to, and presenting to others for their approval and attention, my abstracted thoughts and ideas. This story describes a body that was self-disciplined, neglected, and discriminated against, by both myself and others, in both conscious and unconscious ways.

The second story is, in many respects, a counter-narrative. It is the story of how my body resisted the pressure to disappear, how it pushed for attention and primacy in my experience, and how I alternately supported and refused those impulses. Perhaps more significantly, it is the story of how my body got me to fall in love with it. By extension, this is also the story of how I came to fall in love with the bodies of others.

Although these two stories are being told as if they were separate and opposed narratives (indeed, I have to some extent set them up that way by my earlier reference to the second story as a counter-narrative), in truth, they are inextricably woven together and exist within me in constant and subtle interplay. Both stories can be understood as embodied responses to power; and, like Foucault's understanding of power as a network of relations, these narratives form a web of connections embedded within me in highly visceral yet transmutable ways (Sawicki, 1991). The first story I will tell is a ghost story. Like all ghost stories, death is involved, but in this case the dying is a continuous event. To paraphrase sociologist Chris Shilling (2012), it is the story of the "absent presence" of my body in my life.

I cannot say for certain when I first noticed that my body wasn't there. Certainly, by the age of five (which was when I learned to read), it was absent for long stretches of time. I was immersed in the "life of the mind" in many ways; through stories and music and art, and through sustained and elaborate games of make-believe. Many of these games involved dolls or stuffed animals of some sort, whose plastic bodies became the medium for my imagination and the alternate locus of my identity. I lived through other bodies, not my own. When I gave my own body any thought at all, it was to regard it with a beige indifference.

To outward appearances, I was "fair" in all respects: pale skinned, blue-eyed, blonde, and even featured. While not pretty enough to warrant special attention or privileges, my appearance was certainly acceptable in the culture in which I was born and raised. My physical attributes were "normal" enough for my body to become invisible, to me and to others, and I counted on the cultural currency it offered to have my body not be an issue in nearly any context I chose.

The first time I recall my body failing to serve as adequate cultural currency occurred when I was seven. It was 1967, Canada's Centennial Year, and every public school across the country held physical fitness tests for their students, awarding badges of merit for physical achievement. I was used to excelling at school and looked forward to going to the gym with the rest of the class to participate in the school-wide event. While I have only a vague recollection of the features of the fitness test (push-ups, sit-ups, and the like), I retain a vivid image of the merit badges – gold, silver, bronze, and red – with a stylized centennial maple leaf embroidered on the front. Clearly, the metallic colors echoed the Olympic medals, while the red ones were the badges they gave you just for showing up – in short, for merely *having* a body. It never occurred to me that I wouldn't be able to earn a gold or silver badge, until at the end of my fitness test they handed me a red one.

My reaction that day nearly fifty years ago became the template for all subsequent responses to my body failing to pass the tests society pressed upon it: I was disbelieving, then ashamed, and then resigned. I have kept almost no mementoes of my childhood – no class photographs, no report cards – but I have that little red badge. The implicit message embedded in that red scrap of fabric was clearly inscribed, and it told me that as far as my body was concerned, my contribution to the world was unremarkable.

That initial assessment of my bodily competence was never really challenged as I grew up. I was slow to learn to swim and to ride a bike. I learned to stand on my head, but never mastered the cartwheel. I got chosen somewhere in the middle of the class for softball teams. My father bought me a baseball glove, and tried to teach me how to play, but I threw like a girl. I never did learn how to whistle properly, or snap my fingers. In short, I learned enough for my body to participate fairly competently when I was required to, and never well enough really to want to very much. As a result, I developed a kind of tolerant apathy toward my body that allowed me to push it to the outer margins of my consciousness.

As I write, I am aware of a quiet voice inside that asks about those children whose bodies did not measure up to the social standards required even for participation – kids in wheelchairs, blind kids, fat kids – children for whom even an invitation to join the game would have been remarkable. I recognize the immense privilege inherent in my position, and that even the tolerant apathy toward my body that I have described here is a luxury some cannot afford. Understanding this, I also recognize that this is my story, as I try to tell it as candidly and reflectively as I can.

By the time I was twelve, the disappearance of my body from my life was nearly complete. Aided by the onset of acne and glasses, and the perplexing failure to grow anything much in the way of breasts, I disappeared into music and books. As I retreated from engagement with my own body, I also closed the door to any sensual or visceral engagement with the outside world. The summer I was fourteen, my family drove to the Maritimes on a two-week vacation. My little sister and I sat in the back of the station wagon, reading comics and romance novels the entire trip. After crossing the world's longest covered bridge in Hartland, New Brunswick, without either of us even glancing up at the day's featured scenic attraction, my father turned the car around and drove across it again. This time he insisted that we take our noses out of our books long enough to note the landmark, and we grudgingly complied. I took the disruption as an opportunity to shift my position in the car seat, as my leg had fallen asleep again.

Later that summer, I rode a friend's bicycle down a steep hill wearing nothing but an orange Speedo® swimsuit. I peeled out into a pool of gravel at the bottom, and banged myself up pretty badly in the process. I limped back to my friend's house and huddled on the bathroom floor, while my friend and I waited for our mothers to come home and figure out what to do. I remember vividly how frightened I felt for this injured, traumatized thing that was my body. I was scraped and bleeding, gravel embedded in my flesh from ankle to hip to fingertip. My heart was skittering, and I was on the verge of fainting. When I told my friend that I thought I might pass out (how did I know this, having never fainted before?), she suggested I sit with my head between my knees. I hesitated to disagree with her, since she was older and sounded very sure, but for some reason I insisted that I needed to lie down. I did, and immediately the faintness passed. I felt then the way I have felt many times since, when forced into interaction with a nonverbal alien entity – nursing a sick dog, persuading a frantic squirrel out of my kitchen, or trying to soothe a screaming infant. You know they know something crucial about the situation, but you don't know what it is they know, or if what they want is something with which you would agree. Like a wild animal, my body in the wake of that bicycle accident was a complete stranger to me. As Marcel Proust observed,

> It is in moments of illness that we are compelled to recognize that we live not alone but chained to a creature of a different kingdom, whole worlds apart, who has no knowledge of us and by whom it is impossible to make ourselves understood: our body.
>
> *(Proust, 2005, p. 304)*

After that, my dissociation from my body was intentional, something I pursued as a protective strategy. Not only was my body largely unresponsive to my attempts to direct or understand it, and not very useful in the pursuit of most of the activities I loved, it had also begun to attract negative attention. I tried to dismiss the leering and jeering of eighth-grade schoolboys about the size of my breasts, and ignore the later taunts of "Dyke!" shouted by the cool guys in cars driving past the high school as I walked home. Framing this verbal abuse as a product of small-mindedness only eased part of the sting; the rest was accomplished by framing my body as not very important to my social identity.

By the time I had finished high school and moved away from home, I had slipped into an uneasy truce with my body that involved a fierce addiction to cigarettes, a complex and ambiguous clothing style, and a feigned indifference toward the commodification of my body by others. This indifference manifested itself in sexual relationships that were alternately inhibited and indiscriminate, and was reinforced by living in a subculture of rock music, drugs, and poverty. For the next seven years, I worked an endless series of minimum-wage jobs – short-order cook, salesperson, machine operator, factory worker. My abysmal typing skills and a strong aversion to pantyhose kept me away from the pink-collar office jobs; instead, I found myself neck-deep in work that required me to relate to my body as instrumental, rather than ornamental (a blessing in disguise) or phenomenological (a shame). Granted, most of the work I performed wasn't physically demanding; it simply required me to show up and be a body that could perform routine tasks consistently and fairly competently. I already knew about showing up as a body. After all, I had the red Centennial badge to prove it. Sometimes, however, my body showed up for a task it couldn't handle.

The summer of 1984, I was living in a small town in southern Alberta and took a job working on the line in a factory that made frozen Swedish meatballs. At the head of the assembly line, butchers would hack up pieces of meat and throw them in a grinder where spices and breadcrumbs were added, which then spit the meat out in tiny chunks. The chunks made their way by conveyor belt into a bath of liquid nitrogen that froze them solid. They were then scooped up and shaken into Styrofoam trays, sealed in plastic wrap, and packed into large cardboard boxes each containing twenty-four one-pound trays. My job – at the end of the line – was to pack and seal the boxes, then stack the full boxes onto skids for transfer to storage. My back and arms didn't even last until lunch. I tried to tell the floor manager that the work was too physically demanding, but he couldn't hear me over the noise of the machines, or see me very well through the cold mist swirling from the liquid nitrogen fast-freezer. I walked off the floor and into the employees' change room, got my things out of my locker, and was almost out the door before the floor manager caught up to me. He apologized, and explained that they had never put a girl in that position on the line before. He promised to move me to an easier spot, but I refused to stay. It wasn't just that I was angry at being used without much thought for my bodily welfare; it was that I was ashamed – ashamed that yet again my body wasn't good enough.

I was to revisit this body shame a decade later, when a seemingly innocuous twist of my knee resulted in a chronic injury that, for the next three years, left me unable to navigate stairs or walk distances of more than a hundred yards at a time. At first, I discussed this disturbing new development in my body with as many people who would listen. I underwent a full battery of diagnostic tests, X-rays, and ultrasound procedures. My doctor sent me to an orthopedist, who sent me to a physiotherapist, who prescribed exercises that made my knee worse. I tried cold packs and heat packs, bed rest, and weight training. I taped my knee with duct tape, wore special braces, and orthopedic inserts in my shoes. On the alternative medicine front, I tried acupuncture, movement therapy, and massage. When nothing helped, the care and attention of the medical profession morphed slowly into contempt.

As a patient, I was required to do everything that was asked of me in order to heal my body. I was expected to submit to repeated interrogation, scrutiny, and intervention, and to let strangers touch me in ways I would rather not have been touched. Despite the fact that my medical records were transferred to each new practitioner, I was asked to relate basic information about my condition over and over again. In order to get help, I had to relinquish control over my body, and to frame the story of my injured knee in terms dictated by others.

Up until this point, I was not especially surprised or perturbed by my experience. This is how the Western medical system works, and I had conformed to its parameters countless times before, with barely a twinge of regret. This time was different, however, because this time I didn't get better. As practitioners noted my lack of improvement, they began to insinuate that I was failing to comply with their treatment: "Are you sure you've been doing those exercises like I told you?" Alternately, they suggested that my gullibility in following the recommendations of another (less enlightened) practitioner was the reason for the persistence of my injury: "Well, you do realize that physiotherapists/movement therapists/orthopedists don't really know how to treat this kind of injury, don't you?" Finally, it was implied that I was malingering, and that my knee couldn't really be as painful as I kept saying it was. I was being blamed for the failure of the medical establishment to heal my body, and I spent many months feeling ashamed of my stupid, stubborn, weak, and unreasonable body before I had the good sense to get angry. This experience was to alter forever my stance with respect to the role of medicine and my body.

The second impact of this injury on my sense of my body had to do with the way I moved through the world, how others saw me, and how I came to understand myself in relation to others. The pain in my knee forced me to walk slowly, although I always sped up when I thought I was being watched by others. Walking along the street with a friend or colleague would inevitably raise a silent question to myself about whether I would walk faster than I should to keep up (and pay for it later in pain), or go slowly and bring their unwanted attention to my pace. Even after three years, my partner would dash across the street in traffic, forgetting that I couldn't keep up.

Stairs were another matter entirely. I had to take them one at a time (going either up or down), and support from a handrail was a necessity. Taking the subway during rush hour became an obstacle course in which I fought against the river of quickly flowing bodies to make it safely over to the handrail, while people muttered and pushed past me on their way to get where they were going. I became a slow-moving vehicle pulled over to the right lane on the highway, but without the flashing lights and inverted orange triangle hanging from my rear end. I don't recall feeling overtly targeted by others as a result of my disability, but I can still remember the overwhelming feeling of weakness, smallness, and infirmity. My kinesphere collapsed, my gestures faded into shadows of themselves, and I walked with my head and eyes down. On a purely instinctive, primal level, I felt like I was out of the running in the big race of life.

As I digested the fairly certain knowledge that I would probably never run or dance or jump again, and as I witnessed the impaired interactions of my body with others, I experienced a cascade of surrender in my cells that served as a kind of somatic undertow. I was being dragged down and away from other people, and my body felt powerless to prevent it. When I looked out of my eyes at others, I felt somehow farther away from them than I had been before. My position in relation to the world no longer felt like a matter of strategy or rebellion, or striving for successful interactions. I was cut loose from the herd, and the ties that had bound me to it had unraveled. Initially, this strange dislocation provoked alarm, then depression and apathy. I stopped trying (literally) to keep pace with the world around me, but I had not yet developed another way of being in my body that was not somehow predicated on my relationship to others.

Then, slowly, after several months of resignation and depression, I noticed something else emerge. Although I still felt just as disconnected from the human world, I found myself reorienting to my disabled condition. Gradually, I came to accept my physical pain and limitation as permanent, and stopped struggling to make my body different from what it was. In a world of fiercely ticking purpose, I was a clock unwound, abandoned in the spaciousness of the present moment. With the compelling forces of power in relationship no longer brought to bear, I stopped being motivated by the fear of not being wanted, or of being wanted for the wrong reasons. I was no longer particularly fearful of being used or accused of using. I stopped rushing to advance or defend perceived interpersonal boundaries; instead, I came to rest.

And the place I came to rest in was my body. I started breathing again. I stopped worrying about how I looked to others, and began to move. As I will relate in the counter-narrative that follows, I had long before learned how to be in my body according to my own emergent desires and impulses, but those capacities were reserved for when I was alone, or in the very safe company of kindred spirits. Now I was moving however I felt like moving *in public*. I took up space. I got close when I wanted to, or walked away, or turned my back. I stopped smiling as a social reflex. I stared. I yawned. I touched people; sometimes with affection, and sometimes just out of curiosity. Imagine how you might behave if no one could see you or feel you – if you were a ghost. For me, this meant that I allowed myself far more bodily intimacy and honesty than I had ever thought possible.

Of course, what initially gave me the freedom to live in my body in this way with others was that I didn't care. I was no longer interested in navigating my social interactions in a way that preserved or enhanced my sense of feeling okay in relation to the other person. At that point, I understood myself as essentially powerless, and as someone who would no longer benefit from the kind of power that others could provide – the tribal power to protect, affirm, include, or defend. I had nothing left to gain or lose, which had the effect of making me quietly fearless. Ironically, this was a remarkably powerful position.

The other effect of this severed power relationship with society, and the result-ing descent into my body, was the connection to another source of power. Reconnecting to the authoritative knowledge of my body[1] provided access to a host of resources that had rarely been available to me outside moments of deeply private somatic reflection; increased oxygen, better balance, less muscular strain and tension, more gut instinct. Although the pain in my knee didn't change one whit, I felt awake and grounded and calm.

Over time, I have learned to cultivate this connection to my somatic experience, and to refine how I use it in my interactions with others. I have also become far more attentive to how others bring their bodies to our interactions, listening for the somatic indicators that someone is comfortable or uncomfortable with me, and adjusting accordingly. As might be expected, I have not retained the intensity of stillness or the completely uninvested attitude that initially resulted in the state of embodied fearlessness I have just described. I no longer experience myself as powerless, and there are days when I feel very far from the kind of freedom engendered by that profound dislocation from social expectations and rewards. Despite the fact that I don't live in that state every day, I still remember what it feels like in my body. It remains an indelible point of reference in my life, and I am dedicated to developing the skill, strength, patience, and flexibility to evoke it consistently in my day-to-day interactions with others. It's the way I want to live in my body, and in the world.

Part of what made it possible for me to move more freely in the presence of others in the ways I describe above was the fact that I could draw on a hidden capacity – an underground stream of embodied knowledge cultivated mostly in private, and largely unnamed and unrecognized until then. Despite the fact that I had lived much of my life disconnected from my body (and in some ways, still do), even from a young age something pulled me to attend to my body, to revel in its sensations and pleasures, and to explore its inner kinesthetic and symbolic depths. I understood those experiences as a form of cultural heritage, and the knowledge of my body as a birthright. Although I rarely dared to expose that knowledge to the scrutiny of others, it was something I retained and quietly cultivated while simultaneously becoming more and more dissociated from my body in public settings. What follows, then, is the counter-narrative I promised: the story of how my body got me to fall in love with it, and the gifts of knowledge, presence, and engagement it bestowed.

I learned to dance when I was four. My mom took me to the local YMCA and enrolled me in a creative movement class. Our year-end recital consisted of a bunch of us running around pretending we were angels, dancing between "clouds" that we had formed on the floor with lengths of skipping rope. From that moment, I was hooked. As I got older, I took lessons in jazz and tap before deciding that ballet was my dance form of choice. I was fortunate to have a very accomplished yet gentle woman as my first ballet teacher, and through her I began to see value in a more disciplined approach to movement. Before her, dance was all about expression – now it also began to be about tradition and technique. My respect for ballet as an art form grew in direct proportion to the steepness of my learning curve. I began to realize that although a plié may look like the easiest movement in the world to execute, it takes years to develop the refinement of motor control that allows it to be more than just bending the knees. I began to see the depth, the nuances, and the complexity of an artistic form that previously I had considered simply a marvelous vehicle for my creative urges. Slowly, I began to cultivate the ability to execute movements skillfully and precisely, and to expand my movement repertoire beyond the pedestrian motions of everyday life. The other important discovery I made in my exploration of dance was how central my body was to the experience of bliss. By consciously using my body as the medium for the creative process through dance, I came to recognize a specific state of bodily sensation associated with artistic or creative engagement that I later came to know as *flow*.[2] When I dance, I am powerful, grounded, and utterly myself.

The other positive source of embodied engagement with the world is through my clothes. I have always been something of a quirky dresser; my mom likes to tell me that when I was four I refused to wear anything but pants, and when I was five I refused to wear anything but dresses. Today, I use my clothing consciously as an act of social protest and political resistance. My style is deliberately genderqueer; I now often wear both pants and dresses together as a way to signal to others (and to remind myself) that I refuse the "heterosexual matrix"[3] of gender and sexual orientation that says there are only two mutually exclusive and oppositionally attracted genders. For me, gender is a reiterative performance every time I open my closet to get dressed.

I love that clothes function as powerful but subtle symbols for all kinds of complex cultural ideas. For example, I once taught a graduate class where I asked the students to make observations about me through my clothes. It was very early in the term, and they had not had any opportunity to get to know me through the usual verbal exchange of inquiry and self-disclosure. Despite this, they came up with a number of inspired guesses about my gender identity, socioeconomic class, sexual orientation, personal and political values, and religious affiliation. Just as they might "read" a poem or painting, the students were able to connect the symbols embedded in my clothing to social, cultural, and personal ideas. One student told me that the way I dressed reminded him of a medieval peasant, and that he therefore thought that I must have strong allegiances to the working class. Another guessed that I was a vegetarian and practiced meditation. Many assumed that I was queer, although some confessed to being stumped by some ambiguous markers. When I asked them to identify those markers, they were quickly able to differentiate among very small signals, right down to whether or not I pierced my ears.

Although not all of the "readings" were perfectly congruent with what I had intended to "write" with my clothing, they all revealed some useful facet of the reader and/or the text. Some of the readings actually spoke to an element of my identity that I had not been consciously aware of representing. More significantly for me, one student told me that when she looked at my clothes she started breathing more deeply and her shoulders relaxed. What this suggests to me is that as I use my clothing to induce a particular quality of embodied felt experience in myself, a similar effect can also be conveyed to others. In short, embodied inter-subjectivity extends beyond the skin, to include the modifications of the cultural marker of our body through our clothes, grooming, and bodily adornments.

In this narrative, I relate some of the features of my embodied experience that have a bearing on how I have responded to issues of power and oppression in my life. They include the ways in which gender identity and gender performance have played themselves out through my bodily expression, how social discourse around disability affected the way I took up an injury that impaired my body's mobility and challenged the notion of my body as separate from my identity, as well as how class- and gender-based notions of the body informed my relationship to my body as a worker. I not only discuss the somatic impact of oppression but also describe the ways in which I have learned to use my body as a source of power and creative inspiration in my life, and how it serves as a locus for resisting oppressive social norms and expectations.

Notes

1 The authoritative knowledge of the body is a concept developed by anthropologist Brigitte Jordan (1997), particularly as it relates to women in childbirth.
2 Flow is a concept proposed by psychologist Mihaly Csikszentmihalyi (1997). The flow state is an optimal state of full immersion in the present moment and is characterized by qualities of absorption, engagement, and fulfillment.
3 The heterosexual matrix is a concept articulated by Judith Butler in her book *Gender Trouble* (Butler, 1990).

8

LEARNING FROM THE BODY STORIES

The body stories in the preceding chapters articulate the knowledge and understandings held by individuals who come from diverse cultural and class backgrounds across several generations. Despite our varied life experiences, it is not our experience as "representative" of our "diversity" that is important; these narratives are not meant to speak for everyone in our communities, or to be generalized to others in any particular way. What is salient is that we have each navigated a complex set of events involving the use of power in ways unique to our own dispositions, situations, and range of options. Our bodies have been both formed and informed by these interactions with the social world, and the resulting embodied knowledge has been expressed in part in the narratives.

Taken together, however, these stories underscore the significance of the body as a source and site of social injustice, and provide new insight into the embodied lived experience of oppression. In particular, the narratives illustrate how oppressive interpersonal relations affect nonverbal communication patterns, disrupt healthy boundaries, elicit traumatic reactions, and engender shame. In this chapter, I unpack the somatic experiences of oppression detailed in the narratives and link them to other research findings, anti-oppression theories, and social justice commentaries.

Theme one: intersecting embodied identities

A recurring theme throughout the narratives is the observation by participants that it felt both difficult and unnatural to separate their embodied experiences of oppression into discrete categories that reflected conventional ways of framing social oppression – that is, into specific experiences of racism, sexism, or classism. Nor did participants describe specific forms of oppression as affecting their bodies in unique ways. For example, no one said that only racism (or sexism, or homophobia) contributed to feelings of disconnection from the body. Rather, somatic dissociation and body shame could result from any (or many) of these forms of oppression.

Pat talked about her experience of oppression as "multifaceted and not compartmentalized," and Crissy observed that her experiences of racial oppression always seemed to be inextricably intertwined with gender oppression. She noted how the taunts and teasing of her classmates managed to target her as both aboriginal and female, and how her struggles with body image were related to discrimination that was simultaneously racist and sexist. Zaylie also described the intersecting dimensions of oppression in her observation that, as a black woman dancer, being thinner was a route toward being whiter. She tried to be as thin as possible as a way to minimize the differences between herself and white dancers, and increase her share of the cultural capital afforded by being thin. My own struggles in the meatball factory with class-bound notions of my body as an instrument of labor were also interwoven with a desire to be seen by co-workers as less female (and thereby both more powerful and less available for sexual objectification).

The embodied experiences of oppression described by participants in this study reflect the more complex, nuanced understandings of social oppression put forward by anti-oppressive education theorists such as hooks (1981) and Kumashiro (2000, 2002). They have argued that oppression is always multifaceted, and the related dynamics of "race," gender, culture, and class cannot be separated without risking an oversimplification that neglects to account for the ways in which these various forms of discrimination are mutually reinforcing (Johnson, 2001). Gail Weiss (in Cohen and Weiss, 2003) echoes this complexity when she discusses the role of the body in forming identity, and argues that while the body provides an unconscious, tacit organization to the stories we tell ourselves (and others) about who we are, the "messy" body simultaneously resists our attempts to make those narratives fit within fixed, stable, and discrete parameters. Instead, the findings of this study suggest that it may be more accurate to view the embodied experience of oppression as something held in the body as a complex and painful response to any and all abuses of power (Burstow, 2002). This is not to suggest that, on a body level, all of our experiences of oppression are somehow the same. Our wounds, like our identities, are unique. What we share in common is that the damage has usually been inflicted by a similar set of weapons – for example, those of marginalization, discrimination, blaming, shaming, denial, and the implicit or explicit threat of violence.

The implications of this notion of intersecting embodied identities on embodied social justice work are significant. Following a well-established tradition articulated by Kimberle Crenshaw (1991), who coined the term "intersectionality," and echoed by activists such as Martin Luther King, Jr., bell hooks, Audre Lorde, and many others, the findings of my research suggest that working to end oppression needs to be a collective effort that recognizes the shared pain of injustice across multiple social identifications.

Theme two: embodied microaggressions and asymmetrical interactions

This research study asked participants to describe how they understood the role of their body in navigating power differentials in relationships with others. One of the most striking features of the narratives was the degree to which participants described various features of nonverbal communication in relation to their experiences of oppression.[1] Within this data, several related dimensions emerged:

1. how participants use interpersonal space and other body-based boundary markers to indicate and mediate power dynamics in social interactions;
2. the way gesture and other nonverbal expressions communicate power, privilege, and social standing;
3. how eye contact mediates social relationships; and
4. the use of touch as a nonverbal signal of status and power.

In each case, these nonverbal interactions could be characterized as an embodied form of microaggression. Chester Pierce coined the term "microaggression" as a way to name "subtle, stunning, often automatic, and nonverbal exchanges which are 'put downs'" in describing the daily experiences of African Americans (Pierce et al., 1978, p. 66). The term has since proved so profoundly descriptive of stigmatized people's experiences that it has become centralized in social justice discourse, largely through the contributions of Derald Wing Sue and his colleagues (Sue, 2010; Sue et al., 2007, 2016). Noting that microaggressions may have more negative effects than more traditional and overt forms of marginalization, Sue defines them as "brief, everyday exchanges that send denigrating messages to certain individuals because of their group membership" (Sue, 2010, p. xvi).

I often liken microaggressions to relational paper cuts: they appear small and insignificant, but can be extraordinarily painful; they are often hard for others to see; and the pain sometimes doesn't show up until after the initial incident and then lingers long afterward. The descriptions below help to flesh out how some of the relational damage these microaggressions inflict if enacted through the body.

Navigating body boundaries

All of the participants spoke about the role of the body in navigating interpersonal boundaries, and the ways in which their experiences of oppression affect those navigations. Although each participant experienced these boundaries in a different way, and each made different choices about how to deal with relational invasions and desertions, the body played a key role in these activities. Please note that my use of the term "navigation" here is not intended to imply a sense of agency in these interactions. That is, these experiences of relating to others through the body could just as often be characterized by a sense of partial or impaired capacity to control or mobilize around the interaction. Instead, I use the term to suggest interrelated movement between people in which the outcome of the interaction depends on a number of factors, including the personal and social power attached to the players that informs (and often determines) their movement options.

The most common arena for the embodied navigation of interpersonal boundaries in the data had to do with the physical space between one body and another.[2] Participants cited a number of experiences in which changes in the distance between two people conveyed specific messages about the power dynamics inherent in the interaction. One example is Natalie's story of sitting next to the man on the bus, and how she had literally embodied the gendered message that women shouldn't take up as much space as men. She also talked about walking down the street and feeling that if a group of men are on the same street, that they "own" that space, not her. Crissy related how men have invaded her personal space under the guise of necessity, when men she didn't know situated themselves or moved against her in ways that were unnecessarily intimate in public situations; for example, on the subway or in the grocery store. Natalie's embodied experience of oppression with respect to space also extends to the larger shared space of the natural environment. As a woman, she feels sufficiently unsafe in the unknown and isolated territory of a park or ravine that she dares not take her daily run through them, and she mourns the resulting loss of embodied engagement with the natural environment.

All of the participants spoke in some way to how important it was for them to feel that their boundaries were respected, and that this respect was embodied in the ways others engaged with and navigated their personal space. The narratives also offer examples of creative embodied ways to navigate or protect interpersonal space boundaries. Zaylie noted that she automatically puts more physical space between herself and those she does not perceive as safe, while simultaneously muting her body language to signal that she does not want further contact. Crissy attends to the power relations implied in certain arrangements of bodies, and uses her power as a teacher to support learning in a circle, a spatial arrangement that for her more closely reflects shared power among students and teachers.

Interpersonal boundaries are also expressed in ways other than the use of physical space. Pat described how she unconsciously used her own body weight to provide a buffer between herself and her partner when the relationship provided only blurred and uncertain distinctions between them. She also offered an insightful example of how boundaries can be navigated through the use of eye contact as a boundary regulator, and talked about how she uses her arms and hands to mark the boundaries of interpersonal space between herself and others.

These examples illustrate a form of asymmetrical nonverbal interaction in which participants' understanding of body boundaries caused them to yield space to those with higher perceived status or power. If power equates to territory – as nonverbal communication researchers such as Hall (1963), Henley and Freeman (1995), and Henley (1977) demonstrate it does – then the subjugation of these women occurs on a very literal level, even if the impact sometimes registers below the level of consciousness.[3] The somatic constriction and withdrawal that habitually occur in response to these invasions of personal space also parallel the somatic effects of trauma, which I discuss later in this chapter.

Gesture, posture, and expression

The narratives of the research participants provided rich insights into the ways in which oppression influences how the participants move, gesture, and hold their bodies as a component of nonverbal communication.[4] This sub-theme emerged along several dimensions of experience, but seemed especially relevant with respect to experiences of gender oppression.

Natalie, Pat, and I all described how the social norms that accompanied our identified gender proscribed our movement vocabularies in ways that echo Iris Young's observations about body comportment and gender. In "Throwing Like a Girl," Young (1980) takes up Merleau-Ponty's phenomenology of the body to analyze the ways in which "feminine" body comportment differs from what is considered "masculine." For example, she observes that when a man throws a ball, he puts his whole body and full effort into the motion, while a woman uses comparatively less effort and range of motion.

As a result of embodying the social norms around gender and body comportment, Natalie found that she did not feel free to engage in activities that she might otherwise have embraced. Because she was reluctant to try movements outside the range of what was considered "feminine" due to a fear of how her body would look, she did not try out for the soccer team, or play rough on the school playground. As a result, she speculated that she failed to acquire some of the basic "letters" of the movement alphabet that would have allowed her to form words and phrases that she could then have used to play sports. She further observed that her lessons around body comportment and gender were learned in part the old-fashioned way – through her mother. The intergenerational nature of embodied learning means that women are often taught how to be oppressed (and to oppress ourselves) from the very people who love us, and whom we love.

Pat described a similar effect of oppression on her body comportment as she recalled her experience in physical education class in school. She said that she often felt a lack of confidence in her body, and never felt support from teachers or coaches to stretch her capacities, nor to understand her own intuitive knowing of her body as skillful. The resulting disempowerment had an inhibiting effect on the size and scope of her gestures, and Pat noted that she still becomes self-conscious when she thinks her movements might be seen by others as "too large" or "too expressive." Zaylie described the way in which she modifies her bodily comportment in an attempt to protect herself in difficult or potentially unsafe interactions with others – she deliberately creates more physical space between herself and the source of the threat, and minimizes the scope and intensity of her body language. She gets small and quiet in her body, in much the same way as a prey animal immobilizes itself in the presence of a predator.

A number of participants in the study noted how attentive and attuned they are to the gestures and expressions of others, and attribute this increased sensitivity as a skill that has allowed them to survive social situations in which they have had relatively little power and control. Pat noted that she is especially attentive to the ways in which she uses and reads nonverbal communication, and Crissy described herself as highly sensitive to the nonverbal signals that others give out – whether or not someone smiles or makes eye contact, for example. Zaylie's need to evaluate the gestural communication of others results in very real discomfort when men stand behind her because she feels unable to predict potentially threatening behavior.

These examples of the impact of oppression on gesture and expression echo the early observations by feminist nonverbal communication researchers on dominant/submissive kinesic behavior. Henley's review of the research evidence for sex differences in nonverbal communication patterns concluded that males tended to use gestures and postures suggesting power, while females tended toward movements suggestive of subordination (Henley, 1977).[5]

Eye contact

While not mentioned as frequently as some of the other dimensions of nonverbal communication, both Pat and Natalie made some intriguing observations about the use of eye contact in the navigation of power differentials in interpersonal interactions.[6] Pat described how feelings of shame associated with internalized homophobia resulted in a self-imposed pressure "not to look" at the bodies of others, as if looking at them would signal an interest that might be interpreted by others as inappropriately sexual. She also noted that when she feels really comfortable about being lesbian, she feels more of a right to look at others. In contrast, Natalie described the development of a finely attuned sensitivity to the gaze of others in relation to feelings of disempowerment. She is acutely sensitive to being watched (especially by men), and feels "the frustration of just walking down the street and being aware of men looking at you in a way that doesn't feel comfortable."

These findings are in alignment with nonverbal communication research that states that eye contact is used to discourage or encourage affiliation or attention (Ellyson and Dovidio, 1985), and that eye contact is employed dissimilarly along lines of power difference in social interactions (Henley and Freeman, 1995).[7] Natalie's discomfort when being watched by men may relate to a widely held recognition among nonverbal communication researchers that staring is considered a sign of dominance and possible aggression in both humans and animals (Ellyson and Dovidio, 1985), as may Pat's concern about her own gaze being perceived as intrusive or unwelcome.

Touch[8]

Participants in this study did not talk very much about how touch has formed and informed their understandings of oppression, although several comments are worth noting as they are congruent with nonverbal communication research that suggests that social power confers the right to touch, and that touch is an important non-verbal indicator of the degree of informality or intimacy in a relationship.

For example, Pat's story about sitting with her brother in his backyard and reaching out and touching him on the knee as part of the conversation suggests that, by initiating touch, she was affirming the degree of power she now held in the context of that relationship. Through a simple gesture, she made definitive statements about the mutuality and degree of intimacy she understood their current relationship to reflect, and marked a significant shift in power from what it had been when they were children and he was the more powerful older brother.

This experience of touch contrasts sharply with Pat's negative reaction to a waiter touching her shoulder. In that case, she perceived the touch as inappropri-ately familiar, as did Crissy when someone at a pow-wow touched her hair from behind. In these examples, strangers assumed a "right to touch" based on their readings of the power dynamic of the situation and the bodies within it. It is worth asking if the waiter or the pow-wow dancer would have asserted their relative power in this way if Pat or Crissy had been male, white, or straight.

Crissy noted that she is especially sensitive to issues of space invasion through the use of touch. For example, she always asks before touching someone, and doesn't like it if someone touches her without asking.

To sum up, it is clear from participants' responses that being oppressed has taught them how to pay attention to those components of nonverbal communi-cation that served to reinforce their inferior social status through the nonverbal messages they received from others. They also learned to affirm that status in their responses to those messages, as well as in the messages they themselves transmit.

As Henley and Freeman (1995) suggest in their work on the nonverbal dimen-sions of gender oppression, many of these communication patterns involve asym-metrical interaction or unequal access to certain behaviors. For example, the man sitting next to Natalie on the bus held a degree of social power that afforded him the luxury of taking the physical space to sit comfortably, despite the consequences on Natalie's body of that unequal division of the collective space. Descriptions of the use of gesture, touch, and eye contact also provided examples of this asym-metry based on power difference.

Henley and LaFrance (1984) further suggest that in any situation in which one group is seen as inferior to another, members of that group will be more non-verbally submissive, more readable (nonverbally expressive), more sensitive (accu-rate in decoding another's nonverbal expressions), and more accommodating (adapting to another's nonverbal behaviors). With the possible exception of non-verbal expressiveness (many of the participants in this study spoke about constric-tion in gesture and expressiveness), the findings of this research seem to correlate with the literature.

To put it another way, although it is clear that the people I interviewed for this study experienced embodied microaggressions, they also internalized the nonverbal relational patterns that marked them as socially subordinate and kept them "in their place." Participants took on the body language that they learned was expected of them, to the extent that at least some of the somatic damage they experienced felt self-inflicted. The profound bodily self-monitoring and self-control described by my participants is eloquently echoed in a blog post by Joel Leon in which he enumerates the bodily accommodations he enacts as a black man in relation to white people.[9] For example, he describes walking off the curb to avoid passing too close on the sidewalk, smiling more, minding his hands, sitting "three rows back" in public places, and speaking slowly and quietly. In short, he is careful to minimize his presence in any way possible so white people will have no opportunity to perceive him as a threat.

Nonverbal communication as a locus of social control and a site for resistance

Given the power of nonverbal communication to influence perception and transform meaning, it is perhaps unsurprising the degree to which power dynamics are communicated through this medium. Feminist researchers Jo Freeman and Nancy Henley argue that the nonverbal component of social interaction (rather than institutional structure) is the locus for the most common means of social control (Henley and Freeman, 1995). Members of socially stigmatized groups are constantly reminded of their inferior social status through the nonverbal messages they receive from others. They are also required to affirm that status in their response to those messages, as well as in the messages they themselves transmit. Henley and Freeman assert that the repetitive and insidious nature of these subtle exercises in dominance and submission slip below the level of awareness (if, in fact, they were ever conscious), effectively internalizing social conventions to the point where they may no longer even feel oppressive.

This reiterative feature of nonverbal communication has been extended and radically transformed by poststructuralist feminist/queer theorist Judith Butler through her notion of performativity. In her earlier works, *Gender Trouble* (1990) and *Bodies that Matter* (1993), she puts forward the idea that these repetitive stylized acts are not simply a feature of gender difference, but are constitutive of gender. These actions are not conceived of as conscious or deliberate choices performed by a subject but rather as a "regularized and constrained repetition of norms" that "enables a subject and constitutes the temporal condition for the subject" (Butler, 1993, p. 95).

Butler argues that the categories of sex, gender, and sexuality are culturally constructed through "regulative discourses" (including nonverbal communication as a form of discourse), and it is the repetition of acts shaped by these discourses that maintains the appearance of a coherent (sexual or gender) identity. Of course, because this identity depends on reiteration for its coherence, it is also vulnerable to incoherence and contestation. (If we "are" what we "do," then who are we when we stop doing what we have been doing?) This concept of performativity is at the theoretical center of Butler's work, and could arguably be extended beyond the "doing" of gender to other dimensions of subjective social identity.

There are also important implications for praxis embedded in the notion of performativity: if oppression depends upon naturalized social categories of unequal power and status, the idea that identity is performative (that is, it depends not on natural differences but on reiterative acts) suggests that changing those acts disrupts the categories upon which social inequity depends. By extension, conscious awareness of the nonverbal substrate of interpersonal communication provides a basis for appreciating the role of the body in reproducing these social patterns of inequity and injustice, and suggests particular directions for how the body can be a locus for social and personal change. However, just because certain movements, gestures, or postures are associated with social power, it is important not to suggest that individuals experiencing oppression should automatically adopt those dominant nonverbal patterns. It would be a mistake to assume that such gestures are automatically better, and that it is the oppressed who should change.

Theme three: trauma, oppression, and the body

One of the questions posed by my research was how oppression was experienced interoceptively – that is, on an inner sensing body level. The narratives offer a number of important insights by the participants into the ways in which experiences of oppression have affected the felt sense of their bodies. In particular, participants described experiences that focused on:

- embodied memory;
- somatic vigilance; and
- withdrawal or alienation from the body.

Embodied traumatic memory

Several of the participants offered some insight and understanding into how the body may "hold" or remember experiences of oppression. For example, when I asked Crissy to reflect on the bodily impact of oppression in her life, she offered a vivid description of the sensation of her body being shaken in response to an oppressive experience. Drawing on the implicit knowledge accessed through the Focusing® technique we used in the interview, she talked about feeling as though her body were being violently shaken by an external force, and feeling a "jolt of fear" course through her body. This sensation of being shaken leaves her feeling confused, helpless, and frozen, as if "stuck between fight and flight." Moreover, she noted that these sensations of disruption and disorientation are very familiar to her, and often accompany experiences of being oppressed. By linking this description to the traumatology literature (Rothschild, 2000; van der Kolk, 2015), it is possible to understand Crissy's embodied memory of oppression as resembling the somatic impact of trauma, and exemplifying one aspect of traumatic intrusion, which is characterized by "physiological reactivity on exposure to internal or external cues that symbolize or resemble an aspect of the traumatic event" (American Psychiatric Association, 1994, p. 425).

Pat's explanation of her experience with a Bartholin cyst may also suggest a link between the somatic impact of trauma and oppression. As she described her reaction to having the cyst, Pat spoke about uncovering the deeper symbolic layers of what the cyst represented about her childhood experience and the power imbalance in her relationship with her older brother. She noted how her vagina held a "body memory" of her relationship with her brother that needed to be held until she developed the psychological strength and capacity to look at these particular issues of gender oppression. By focusing on the felt experience of her body, she was able to access layers of early grief and loss that were "laid down in the body." While Pat's training as a psychotherapist has provided her with a conceptual framework for making the links between trauma and the body, it was in relation to my asking about the effects of oppression on her body that she offered this example. Further, she clearly indicated that she understood it as a form of embodied memory, and as a symbolic somatic manifestation of an earlier traumatic wounding.

Another example of the impact of oppression on the felt experience of the body was provided by Zaylie's recounting of her experience when engaging in the Focusing® exercise during our second interview. She noted that "there was this kind of tar coating all of my insides that was stopping me from absorbing anything. Like everything that would come into me would just pass through." She described this tarry substance as something she ingested from the outside world, and that now exists within her body as the residue of her experiences of oppression. She further acknowledged that this residue prevents her from absorbing emotional, psychological, and relational nutrients – in short, from being affected by positive experiences with others. It is not just that her body lives with the residual effects of oppression, but that oppression interferes with her capacity to engage with and be nourished by the world.

Although Zaylie did not describe this experience as an intrusive traumatic memory, it is clear from her description that repeated experiences of oppression have left an imprint on the felt experience of her body that could be understood as a form of damage. This echoes Burstow's assertion that trauma is a reaction to a kind of wound, and that the physicality of trauma must be recognized even when no overt bodily assault occurs (Burstow, 2003). Recent research into the somatic effects of trauma (Ogden et al., 2006; van der Kolk, 2015) underscores the role of the body in mediating traumatic experiences, and the participants' descriptions of their embodied experience of oppression provides important insights into how oppression as a form of trauma may be held and remembered in the body.

Somatic hypervigilance

All of the research participants spoke about how highly sensitized and attuned they feel to the reactions and responses of others, and although their narratives also describe the ways in which they now take advantage of this heightened awareness in a positive way, it was clear in my conversations with them that their relational sensitivity was initially borne of necessity resulting from painful and challenging experiences with others.

In her narrative, Zaylie referred to a type of somatic hypervigilance with respect to men, and spoke about needing to be able to read their nonverbal communication, especially when in close physical proximity. Given that she also named sexism and sexual assault by men as part of her experience of oppression, it is not surprising that her vigilance is oriented to them as a potential threat. Natalie also made reference to her vigilance in noticing men in her environment, and noted her discomfort as something felt in her body. Pat observed that she is especially attentive to the bodily dimension of interpersonal interaction, and acknowledged that she becomes increasingly self-conscious when she feels that others do not respond to her nonverbal cues with some degree of kinesthetic empathy. As a young child, Crissy's somatic vigilance was focused on her mother, and her narrative describes the ways in which she learned to be highly attentive to her mother's smallest nonverbal cues in order to help her anticipate and avoid an angry outburst of verbal abuse. This increased alertness to the body signals of others has continued into adulthood, and Crissy noted that she remains highly sensitive to nonverbal indicators from others that might suggest interpersonal conflict or difficulty.

Since human somatic responses to danger (even when that danger is not necessarily physical) are hard-wired into our autonomic nervous systems (Porges, 2011; van der Kolk, 2015), it makes sense that participants reported feeling increased body alertness around sources of potential harm, whether that source is a group of men standing on a street corner or a conference table full of white, middle-class professionals. The experiences of participants as related in their narratives illustrate the ways in which this somatic vigilance became established for them as a habitual pattern of response. Although the catalysts for this response are experiences of oppression, the participants' descriptions of the response itself are similar to those found in post-traumatic stress (American Psychiatric Association, 2013).

Somatic withdrawal and alienation

In describing the somatic impact of oppression, all of the participants spoke about the profound disconnection from the felt experience of their bodies. In many cases, this disconnection was something that participants had realized only recently, through the process of addressing the impact of oppression. At the same time, participants also described this withdrawal from the felt experience of the body as strategic – something that allowed them to survive the painful feelings generated by their experiences of oppression.

Pat spoke about the experience of somatic disconnection at some depth, and noted that her regaining of body awareness has proved crucial to her healing and empowerment. She described the inability to inhabit her body fully as one of the core pieces of traumatic fallout, and a "certain state of collapse" in her body that reflected a similar state of collapse in her psyche. At the same time, her use of various bodily mediated substances – smoking, alcohol, food – can also be interpreted as coping strategies that induce the desired effect of bodily detachment and numbing. Crissy's elaboration of her years of drug and alcohol abuse echo a similar strategy. Interestingly, Zaylie described a learned dissociative strategy through the process of education, in her description of dissociation as explicitly taught in "white" dance.

From my own narrative, an understanding of the role of somatic dissociation as a protective mechanism in response to traumatic oppression centers on the premise that the interaction between myself and my environment is rooted in survival. Both physically and psychologically, I depend on being able to access the shared resources of the social and natural environments to meet my needs, and my life energies are directed toward making those interactions successful. My experiences of oppression, and the resulting traumatic responses of dissociation and constriction, could be understood as unsuccessful interactions with the social environment. Despite the frustration of being unable to meet my needs to be included and acknowledged without overt or implied negative judgement, my reaction to that frustration has been to withdraw and recoup my energies for the next interaction. On rare occasions, my response would be more extreme, and I would question the value of continuing to attempt some kind of satisfying overall relationship, and stay in the outer margins for as long as I possibly could. This could be understood both as a strategic retreat prior to reengagement and as deliberate disenfranchisement. It is important to note that, for me, this withdrawal and alienation occur on both a somatic and a social level; that is, my feelings of disconnection from the felt experience of my body usually coincide with similar feelings of disengagement with the body politic.

The descriptions of somatic withdrawal and alienation provided by the participants appear to correlate in some way to the post-traumatic stress disorder avoidance criteria described in the trauma literature (American Psychiatric Association, 2013). These criteria include feelings of detachment from self and others, which on a body level relates to what Nijenhuis (2000) and others describe as somatic dissociation. In many cases, this disconnection was something that participants realized only in retrospect, through the process of addressing the impact of oppression. At the same time, participants also described this withdrawal from the felt experience of the body as initially functional; that is, as something that allowed them to survive the painful feelings generated by their experiences of oppression.

The trauma literature suggests that, on a somatic level, the dissociative mechanism that serves to protect the individual from distressing material may also serve to disconnect them from a general sense of kinesthetic awareness (van der Hart et al., 2001; Waller et al., 2001). This altered state of consciousness provoked by traumatic stress is one in which the traumatized individual does not experience bodily sensations fully or accurately, and this lack of fundamental connection to the physical self may produce a range of secondary effects – distorted body image, distorted awareness of physical space boundaries, and poor movement coordination (Blume, 1990).

The experiences described in the narratives also brought to mind the work of McKinley and Hyde (1996) on objectified body consciousness, which suggests that systemic oppression and socially constructed imperatives about the body combine in ways that support marginalized subjects to experience their bodies from the outside, rather than from within. Laura Doyle (2003) further suggests that traumatic oppressions, such as racism, work to unhinge corporeal self-relation and produce an alienated subjectivity. According to Doyle, the social world colonizes our bodily selves and then refuses us admission, so that access to our own bodily experience must be filtered through the lens of those colonizing others. Regaining this lost access to the breathing, sensing, knowing self lies at the heart of an embodied approach to social justice.

Connecting the dots between trauma and oppression

There is a growing body of literature linking oppression and trauma, and researchers have begun to recognize microaggressions against marginalized people as a form of trauma. For example, in a departure from the conventional understanding of trauma as a single life-threatening incident, Mol et al. (2005) compared post-traumatic stress disorder (PTSD) scores from more than 400 participants who experienced single traumatic events with an equal number of participants who experienced prolonged life-stressors. They found that individuals with prolonged stressors actually had more reported PTSD symptoms – hypervigilance, arousal, and avoidance – than those who experienced acute traumas. Similarly, Scott and Stradling (1994) provide numerous examples of PTSD in members of oppressed groups who show full symptomatology in the absence of a single acute trauma.

Increasingly, oppression is being understood as a prolonged life-stressor, to the extent that Kira et al. (2013) define it as a collective trauma perpetrated between groups that exists on a continuum from microaggressions to macroaggressions. In a sample of Palestinian youth, these researchers found that such oppression directly predicted collective group identity salience, and that it was significantly associated with increased PTSD symptoms, suicidality, depression, and anxiety. Bryant-Davis and Ocampo (2005) found similar trauma symptoms between survivors of racist incidents and survivors of sexual and domestic violence, while Walters and Simoni (2002) contend that discrimination against Native American women partially accounts for their high rates of PTSD and trauma-related symptoms. Likewise, Kira et al. (2012) found that gender discrimination significantly accounted for the variance in type and severity of trauma symptoms between male and female survivors of torture. In their sample, sexist microaggressions against women significantly increased the severity of PTSD symptoms and their overall susceptibility to subsequent trauma.

Many traumatologists now recognize trauma as a neurophysiological as well as a psychosocial experience (Levine, 1997; Ogden et al., 2006; Rothschild, 2000; van der

Kolk, 2015) and agree that "traumatic events exact a toll on the body as well as the mind" (Rothschild, 2000, p. 5). Somatic scholar Don Hanlon Johnson suggests that the legacy of trauma is perhaps most strongly felt in our bodies, and the massive global incidence of war, politically directed torture, famine, rape, and domestic violence indicates a "criminal disregard for the muscle fibers, fluids, and neural networks in which we live" (Johnson, 1995, p. ix).

Within the field of trauma research, the somatic effects of trauma have now been well documented, including neurobiological changes (alterations in brainwave activity, in the size of brain structures, and in the functioning of processes such as memory and fear response) and psychophysiological changes (hyperarousal of the sympathetic nervous system, increased startle response, sleep disturbance, and increased neuro-hormonal changes that result in heightened stress and increased depression) (van der Kolk, 2015).

Given the increasing evidence from the traumatology literature, and in alignment with the findings of my own research, it seems clear that understanding and working with the traumatic impact of oppression requires an appreciation and recognition of these somatic effects as well as for the cognitive and emotional symptoms of post-traumatic stress.

Theme four: body image and body shame

Another key theme emerging from the narratives concerns how experiences of oppression have shaped participants' body image.[10] The descriptions of these experiences fall across three related dimensions:

- issues related to body weight and fat oppression;
- issues related to skin color and racism; and
- issues concerning physical attractiveness, appropriateness, and competence.

Body weight

Crissy's description of her struggle with an eating disorder perhaps best exemplifies how powerful the cultural messages to be thin really are. In addition to having to deal with pervasive social norms that devalue fat women, the prevailing prejudice in Crissy's community of peers was that aboriginal women tended to be large, effectively linking her body size with her aboriginal heritage. Crissy's attempts to make herself less noticeably aboriginal by staying thin evolved into a serious pattern of laxative abuse, as her physical appearance came to represent the primary source of "what was wrong" with her.

Although feminist theorists and the popular media often represent body image issues primarily as a facet of gender oppression (McKinley, 1998), Crissy and Zaylie both made connections between body image and racism. In both cases, thinness was understood by them to be equated with whiteness, and pursuit of the idealized body image became not only a route toward acceptance and desirability as a woman, but a way to avoid or offset racial prejudice and discrimination.

The concerns Pat and Natalie expressed with respect to weight also reflect prevailing gender-oppressive imperatives on women to limit and control their body size. Pat described the challenges of growing up feeling as though she was always overweight, and working through the resulting feeling of internalized shame in which her body is never going to be "okay." Although Natalie acknowledged that she has always been slender, she noted that fat oppression has had a strong impact on her. Even as a young child, she understood how much cultural capital her slim figure afforded her, both in her mother's eyes and in the eyes of others. She came to view her own thinness as something that was a critically valuable aspect of her identity, and fat oppression became a mechanism by which she was encouraged to view her body as an object whose appearance must conform to external expectations and desires.

Skin color

The narratives suggest that skin color is a complex source of body image concerns. Crissy, Zaylie, and Natalie all spoke about how their skin color is used by others to frame them as unacceptably different, although these frames of reference seem highly variable and contextually dependent. For example, Zaylie notes that she is sometimes seen as black, and sometimes not. Understandably, the impact of skin color on their body image has also varied. Crissy spoke about wanting to be both lighter-skinned and darker-skinned, depending on her social environment and on her own developing attitudes toward racism. For Natalie, being white also became a source of body shame when a key social environment excluded her from membership because of her skin color.

In some respects, these observations suggest what critical race theorists Delgado and Stefancic (1997) observe in their assertion that "race" (and thereby racism) seems to be largely relational. That is, "whiteness" serves as a social norm against which all other characteristics of skin color are judged. In relation to whiteness, both Zaylie and Crissy are subjected to racism because of the color of their skin, regardless of the fact that they are both of mixed "racial" background. At the same time, they can also be subjected to discrimination based on skin color when their relative whiteness is viewed with disdain or suspicion by those who identify as "non-white."

Appropriateness, competence, and attractiveness

While body image concerns in relation to body weight and skin color were emphasized in conversations with the participants in this study, other facets of body image were also discussed. For example, Pat remarked that her primary sense of her body has always been that she will fail or look foolish, and that she grew up feeling that her body somehow wasn't good enough. This failure of her body to meet social expectations was related to physical competence (such as doing well in gym class) as well as to gender presentation. She implicitly understood that in order to be accepted by her family, her body's inherent "tomboy" qualities would have to be masked by grooming and clothing strategies that disguised them under a veneer of stereotypical femininity.

The pressure Pat felt to conform to accepted standards of gender presentation echoes the observations of feminist theorists who note that embodiment has been characterized by binary norms – male/female, well/ill, heterosexual/homosexual, black/white – and that these norms are both threatened and confirmed by the existence of bodies that fall outside them (Butler, 1990; Grosz, 1994). Many feminists would also argue that women have usually paid the higher price to have bodies that are visible as stereotypically feminine (Price and Shildrick, 1999). Elaborating on the insights of Michel Foucault on the role of surveillance in reinforcing social body norms, Susan Bordo (1993) and Sandra Bartky (1989) have argued that diet, fitness, fashion, and healthcare all serve as disciplinary controls that not only direct our choices, but actively construct our notions of what the body is.

In my own narrative, I discuss how chronic injury reinforced perceptions of my body as shameful, incompetent, and powerless. As a patient, I was required to do everything that was asked of me by the medical authorities: to submit to repeated interrogation, scrutiny, and intervention; to let strangers touch me in ways I would rather not have been touched; to relinquish control over my body; and to relate the story of my disability in terms dictated by others. The subsequent failure of the medical establishment to "cure" me was framed as a failure of my body, and initially provoked both body shame and alienation. Echoing Laura Doyle (2003), the sociologist Arthur Frank (1996) argues that the modernist conception of illness is a form of "colonization" in which the ill or injured person surrenders their body to biomedical expertise. Critical disability theorists, such as Eli Clare (2001) and Robert McRuer (2003), further assert that bodies whose characteristics fall outside the norm are often seen as sick and wrong.

Crissy's self-described battle with acne also reveals how the medicalization of certain body conditions frames them as disorders and obscures the social stigmatization at the root of much medical discourse. Her narrative further illustrates the sophisticated double-bind that perpetuates body shame: if Crissy does nothing about her acne, she feels ashamed of how she looks; but if she treats her acne with interventions that put her health at risk, she feels ashamed of being vain.

Social theorists Giddens (1990), Shilling (2012), and others provide a basis in the literature for understanding the stories related by participants with respect to how their bodies look in comparison to perceived social norms and expectations. They argue that, due to the loss of more established social structures upon which to base our sense of selfhood, the exterior of the body has become one of the few remaining constant "structures." As a result, increasing social attention is being placed on the body as an expression of individual identity, and it becomes increasingly important as a social symbol that gives signals to others about who we are (Bourdieu, 1980; Goffman, 1959; Shilling, 2012).

Many critical social theorists understand these differences as strategies of oppression (Butler, 1990; Cohen and Weiss, 2003; Price and Shildrick, 1999). They argue that the surface of the body features prominently in the articulation of social difference, and is therefore an important basis for social oppression, as well as a potential site for resistance.

Wearing our identities

This section discusses how the bodies of participants serve as a site for the elaboration of identity with respect to issues of oppression through clothes, grooming, and other symbolic indicators. Like the body itself, the objects that adorn the body communicate powerful nonverbal messages that add significantly to the lexicon of body language. Although the particular codes for reading these symbols vary across a range of social identities and affiliations – gender, class, income, occupation, ethnic and religious background, marital status, and sexual orientation, for example – the relationship between body symbols, power, and social identity can be profound, and our body adornments serve as compelling markers of who we are.[11]

Clothing as a form of nonverbal object communication was mentioned several times throughout the narratives as playing a part in body image as related to issues of oppression. These findings support the notion from the nonverbal communication literature that clothes function as powerful but subtle symbols for all kinds of complex cultural ideas (Corrigan, 1992). For example, Pat's noted ambivalence about clothes and grooming that negate or obscure the complexity of her gender identity illustrates how dressing to "fit in" has both social benefits and hidden personal costs. While she wanted to convey an appropriately professional image in her work situation, the messages about gender that these clothes also conveyed (e.g., pantyhose and heels) did not reflect Pat's personal affiliations around gender (e.g., her "tomboy" side).

She also spoke about how early imperatives around clothing and grooming affected her body image. As a young girl, Pat constantly received messages from her mother and others about grooming, dress, and appearance that related only to social expectations. She learned how to "accentuate my good features" and comply with expectations about how females present their bodies in social situations. Significantly, she remembered feeling these injunctions had almost nothing to do with who she really was, and that her own creativity around personal image through the use of body symbols was imperceptibly but persistently discouraged. In this way, those with more power had the right to dictate the identity of someone with less power by limiting their choices around personal expression through body symbols as object communication.

While the social imperatives around presentation taught to Pat centered largely on gender norms, Natalie observed that clothing as an element of body image also has class attributes. Her description of how she would sometimes dress up to go shopping in order to get better service (i.e., to draw on the cultural capital that certain clothing affords) acknowledges how she has used it as a way to transform her body image to acquire social benefits. It also reflects an evolving shift (Shilling, 2012) toward the body as ornamental rather than instrumental.

My own observations on the role of clothing as reproducing and potentially disrupting oppressive social relations are noted in my narrative. I use clothing as an act of social and political resistance, and as a way to reclaim my body image from the prevailing hegemonic discourse that presses me to conform to a pre-scribed/proscribed set of images. Although Butler (1990) argues that performativity with respect to gender is not necessarily a conscious or deliberate act, I draw on her idea that gender is a reiterative performance every time I open my closet to get dressed.

Of course, clothing is not the only form of body-based object communication that speaks to issues of social power. Crissy's description of how she cut her hair very short during a time in her life when she was feeling "unclean" speaks to how it served as a powerful but complex body symbol. Cutting her hair was both an expression of how powerless she felt and an attempt at bodily decontamination. When she decided to cut her hair in her early twenties, she was speaking to the many layers of experience that are encoded within the symbolic representation of our bodies – what it meant to her to be aboriginal, female, young, and struggling with power.

Theme five: body knowledge and power

Despite the embodied wounds inflicted over a lifetime of unjust and inequitable power relations, each of the participants in this study also experiences her body as an important source of knowledge and power, and as a site for resisting and unlearning oppression. Although safely regaining access to this source of power often required the same patient creativity that Laura Doyle (2003) describes in her analysis of embodiment and slavery, each of them recognized the importance of doing so.

For Zaylie and Crissy, dance forms that reconnect them with their cultural heritage provide a medium for embodied expression that helps them reclaim the power of their bodies for themselves. Zaylie noted that dance (and "black" dance forms in particular) provides her with an extensive movement vocabulary, and that she consciously uses her learned capacity to articulate concise nonverbal messages as a way to resist or deflect oppression.

For Natalie, yoga provides a means of connecting with her body in a gentle and compassionate way that helps to soften some of the critical voices that have become embedded in her body image over the years. Crissy's movement classes serve a very similar purpose, and allow her not only to engage with her body in positive ways, but to facilitate that engagement for others. Pat and Natalie both acknowledge that finding ways to experience themselves as athletically capable has helped to foster a growing sense of their bodies as powerful, although it is perhaps worth noting that neither has yet chosen to undertake this reclamation through team sports.

For me, reclaiming my body as a source of creative power has taken many routes, including dance and other forms of artistic expression. The experiences I relate in my narrative could perhaps best be described using the lexicon of humanistic psychology. For example, psychologist Abraham Maslow would likely understand my experience of embodied power as a peak experience (or something approaching one), while Csikszentmihalyi (1997) might call it flow (Privette, 1983). Buddhists might call this experience "waking up," in reference to its particular qualities of clarity, energy, and engaged yet broadened perspective.

In nearly every case, this reclaiming of the body as a source of personal and social power seems to have evolved through a process of intuitive selection and fortunate circumstance. In all cases, it has also proceeded through a process of education, whether that learning occurs independently and informally or through more established frameworks. However, except for Zaylie (whose capacity for embodied knowledge has been consistently cultivated over many years of movement training), the way back to the body has not been an obvious or easily accessible path. Certainly, the participants acknowledged that safe forums for such explorations are rare, and that public education systems have not been sites for reclaiming their bodies as primary sources of experience, knowledge, and power.

Implications for embodied social justice

Unpacking the body narratives of my research participants allows their insights to be linked to the knowledge generated by social science research across a range of disciplines, including anthropology, psychology, traumatology, and cultural studies. The five themes generated by the narratives underscore the role of the body as a site of social injustice and resistance, and illustrate the degree to which oppressive interpersonal relations distort nonverbal communication, elicit traumatic somatic reactions, and engender body shame.

To sum up, the implications of my research for social justice theory and practice include the following:

1. The complex nature of embodied responses to oppression requires working intersectionally and collaboratively, rather than only in issue-specific groups.
2. Social justice work needs to support individuals to take embodied micro-aggressions seriously, and to understand themselves as both victims and perpetrators. Similarly, it is important to help illuminate our participation in dominating and self-subordinating movement patterns, and to acknowledge their impact on our bodily experience of self and others.
3. Social justice activists need to learn to recognize the somatic indicators of oppression-induced trauma in themselves and others. In particular, strategies for regaining access to the sensing, feeling, and knowing body must be cultivated.
4. In order to reclaim the body as a source of knowledge and power in social justice work, issues of body shame and somatic illiteracy must be identified and addressed.

In Part II, I review some of the scholarly and professional work being under-taken to address these issues, and note the need for an integrative framework. In Part III, I describe a model of embodied social justice work that incorporates these findings into a comprehensive strategy for disrupting how our bodies become implicated and coopted into reproducing oppression.

Notes

1 Communication between human beings is a complex, dynamic, contested, con-tingent, and contextually dependent system. It involves all modes of sending mes-sages and receiving feedback, and draws on innate reflexive characteristics as well as socially learned behaviors. Nonverbal communication can be broadly defined as all of the messages – other than words – that people exchange in the course of their interactions with one another. At times, nonverbal cues are used to modify or underscore a verbal message, while on other occasions they replace verbal commu-nication (Burgoon et al., 2016). Although these nonverbal dimensions of commu-nication are rarely an explicit focus when communications are reviewed or analyzed, their significance to the overall message is considerable. Anthropologist Ray Bird-whistell (1970) claimed that about two-thirds of a message's meaning is commu-nicated through these nonverbal clues, while Mehrabian (1971), and Fromkin and Rodman (1983) assert that up to 90 percent of the emotional meaning of a message is transmitted nonverbally. Although some experts in nonverbal communication argue that this latter figure is exaggerated, most concur with Birdwhistell's estimate (Hickson et al., 2003). The importance of nonverbal communication is further demonstrated by the finding of Argyle (2013) that nonverbal cues have over four times the impact of verbal cues when both are used together. Nonverbal commu-nication experts assert that nonverbal communication affects our relationships and interpersonal environments in intricate ways, providing insight into emotional states, and influencing perceptions of competence, sincerity, authority, and vulnerability. Given the acknowledged significance of the nonverbal aspect of interpersonal com-munication, it makes sense to attend to it as a crucial component of power relations between people.

2 "Proxemics" refers to the study of our perception and use of interpersonal space. The term was coined by anthropologist Edward T. Hall (1974) to describe the measurable distances between people as they interact. He observed that individuals unconsciously establish a comfortable distance for different types of personal interaction and non-verbally define this as their personal space: intimate distance for embracing, touching, or whispering; personal distance for interactions among close friends; social distance for interactions among acquaintances; and public distance used for public speaking. Chan-ging the distance between two people can convey a desire for intimacy, declare a lack of interest, or increase/decrease domination; and violation of this personal space can have serious adverse effects on communication. Like the other types of nonverbal commu-nication, the use of space varies across culture, gender, age, and other social factors.

3 Early studies in nonverbal communication (Sommer, 1969) showed that dominant ani-mals and high-status human beings are afforded greater personal space, and those with lower status tend to yield space to those with higher status.

4 Kinesics is the study of nonverbal communication related to movement of any part of the body, or the body as a whole. The meanings communicated through body move-ments vary widely – cultural and gender differences in gestures are remarkable, and there is no "international language" of gestures. Instead, cultures have developed systems of unique gestures, so it is almost never possible to understand intuitively the gestures from

another culture. To offer some idea of how kinesic behavior related to cultural and power difference might come into play in an educational context, Vargas (1986) notes a study in which black students perceived that they were being "talked down to" by their white educators. Where white students would nod and murmur "uh-huh" as new information was explained, black students in the research appeared to nod less perceivably and use "mhm" as a regulator utterance. Vargas concluded that because black students made different use of kinesics than white students, white teachers thought black students did not understand what was being said to them, and overexplained, resulting in a student perception of patronization.

5 Later feminist theorists would complexify and problematize such an essentialized notion of gender. For example, queer theorist Judith Butler (1990, 1993) provides a key concept in understanding how bodies are implicated not only in the social production of gender difference, but in notions of identity. Butler formulated a conception of the body that centers on the ideas of performance and reiteration; through her notion of *performativity* (identity as constructed through a process of reiterative acts and gestures), gender shifts from being comprised mostly of nouns to becoming significantly about verbs.

6 "Oculesics" is the term used to refer to the study of the use of the eyes and eye movement. This includes eye contact (or the avoidance of it) as well as other eye movements, such as looking at parts of the other person, or at other features of the environment. For example, research suggests that the eyes have directive features – when a speaker suddenly looks to the side of the room, her observers often look there, too. Eye movement and eye contact are also used to discourage or encourage affiliation or attention (Ellyson and Dovidio, 1985). Like other nonverbal communication, the way in which the eyes are used to convey particular messages varies across cultures.

7 Eye contact appears to be employed dissimilarly along lines of power difference in social interactions. Researchers have found that both men and women will look more at those they regard as sources of social approval, and that women (as might be expected, given their subordinate social status) look more at another person in a dyad than men do (Hall and Halberstadt, 1986; Ellyson and Dovidio, 1985). Henley and Freeman (1995) conclude that looking is suggestive of dependency and subordination, and that although women may watch men when they are not being looked at, they lower or avert their gaze when a man looks at them, as submissive animals do when a dominant animal looks their way. Staring, however, is widely believed to communicate aggression and dominance in both humans and animals (Ellyson and Dovidio, 1985).

8 "Haptics" is the term that nonverbal communication researchers use to refer to touching behavior. Although most frequent during greetings and departures (e.g., handshakes, kissing, hugging), touching can occur throughout an interaction. Haptic behavior is often an indicator of the degree of informality or intimacy in a relationship. The boundaries between different degrees of intimacy may change from one individual to the next, and across cultures. Remland et al. (1995) recorded the touching behavior of a number of different groups of people while communicating. They found that in England, France, and the Netherlands touching was relatively rare, compared to their Italian and Greek samples. In many Arabic countries men frequently touch each other in public or walk arm-in-arm down the street. The use of touch also varies according to gender and age (women and children are touched more than adult males).

9 Available at: www.bdcwire.com/things-i-do-for-white-people/, accessed March 29, 2017.

10 Our capacity to shape our bodies through body projects that simultaneously modify our social relations is reflected in a wide array of practices, from what we wear and how we groom ourselves through to exercise, diet, bodywork, pharmaceutics, and cosmetic surgery (Shilling, 2012). These body practices become part of a lifestyle – a "relatively integrated set of practices chosen by an individual in order to give material form to a particular narrative of self-identity" (Shilling, 2012, p. 181). According to many social theorists (Foucault, 1990, 1991, Turner, 2008; Shilling, 2012; Mauss, 1979), the body is an increasingly critical and recurring theme in that narrative. The role that somatic

awareness can play in altering the body project is discussed in more detail in the section on reclaiming body image in Chapter 13.

11 A comprehensive introduction to the sociology of clothing is not possible here, but the interested reader might begin with Corrigan's work on the socio-semiotics of clothing (Corrigan, 1992). For the purposes of this book, clothing is understood as an extension of the body; as its "second skin." Like the body, clothing communicates powerful nonverbal messages whose particular codes vary across time and culture. As with other mediums of communication, these messages may be interpreted (or misinterpreted) in terms of a range of social identities and affiliations, and they have particular implications for social power differentials. For example, Veblen (1899) maintained that dressing for status provided an effective mechanism for maintaining class boundaries due to the fact that the restrictive design of high-status clothing prevented the wearer from engaging in manual labor, and required the assistance of servants to dress the wearer and maintain the garments. The design of women's clothing in Europe and North America continues to serve a similar purpose with respect to gender difference, consistently emphasizing ornamentality over functionality. More recently, racial discrimination based on clothing found expression in the so-called Zoot-Suit Riots in Los Angeles during World War II (Mazon, 2002).

PART II
Oppression and embodiment

9

(UN)LEARNING OPPRESSION

In Chapter 1 of this book, I described some of the professional challenges that catalyzed my decision to focus on how the lived experience of the body is affected by (and implicated in) oppressive social relations. In nearly thirty years of clinical practice, I have witnessed oppression's corrosive effects on the resilience and generativity of countless individuals across multiple contexts: women in addiction treatment centers; elderly black men in psychiatric hospitals; children with autism; immigrants in homeless shelters; and queer youth in crisis. In every case, the painful life circumstances of these individuals were either caused or exacerbated by the discrimination, marginalization, and abuse they suffered as a result of being marked as a member of a socially subordinated group.

Given the myriad categories, imperceptible degrees, and picayune excuses for treating others as inferior based on an arbitrary set of characteristics, most of us can understand this pain on a personal level as we've experienced it in some form or other. In teaching the topic of embodied social justice to graduate students over the past decade, I have also come to realize that even those whose bodily characteristics mark them as privileged (young, white, male, and able-bodied, for example) often carry some hidden pain. Perhaps they were chubby as a child, or have lost the ability to cry. Perhaps their social status has so inured them to the plight of others that they struggle to form intimate and meaningful relationships. The point here is not to absolve people from owning the impact of their social power, but to recognize that, understood from an intersectional perspective,[1] most of us hold privilege in some contexts and suffer some disadvantage in others. To varying degrees, we know what it's like on both sides of the oppression coin.

What this means is that social justice work is not just for "minorities" struggling to secure basic human rights (although it *is* that). It means that this work is for everyone, regardless of our professional affiliations or personal circumstances. Every day, each one of us has an experience that has been shaped by prejudice and bias.

Most of us have recurrent interactions that are much less satisfying than they could be because social norms and expectations have distorted our ability to make genuine contact with ourselves and others. We are all impoverished by the limits on community imposed by unnecessary barriers that divide us according to "race," class, age, gender, ability, and other perceived features of bodily and behavioral difference.

The pervasive and persistent fact of oppression has given rise to numerous philosophies, approaches, and models designed to help understand and disable its mechanisms and to address its impact. Some of these models are intended for use by communities wanting to take action around a particular social issue. Gandhi's nonviolent action model is a good example, where multiple strategies (such as boycotts, protests, and picketing) are employed within a clear set of ideological and practical guidelines. Other approaches have been developed for use in business and nonprofit organizations (for example, cultural competence models that define and set standards for multicultural diversity and inclusion practices among members). The model introduced in this book is designed specifically for those in the helping professions (including human service professionals, counselors, educators, social workers, and healthcare practitioners) whose work requires them not only to deliver services in a culturally competent way but to help facilitate positive change in the lives of clients and students around issues of oppression.

To develop the conceptual frame[2] that grounds the research upon which this book is based, I drew on the work of scholars in philosophy, psychology, sociology, anthropology, and cultural studies. Each, in their own way, made important contributions to our understanding of the body in relation to human experience, as well to our understandings of knowledge, power, and social justice. However, the model itself is rooted directly in experiential learning theory, and in the critical and embodied approaches to teaching and learning developed by somatic and anti-oppression educators.

As I noted in the Chapter 1, I chose to work with a learning model (rather than a healing/therapeutic model or a social action model) for many reasons. One reason had to do with accessibility: I recognized that many of the people who might use this model would not necessarily be trained and licensed to provide psychotherapeutic services; nor would they necessarily hold leadership roles as community activists. I also understood that many members of oppressed groups might (for very good reasons) resist working in a way that suggested that they were psychologically damaged and in need of healing. I hoped that framing the individual and collective transformation of oppression as a learning process might be more appealing.

But the main reason I ground my approach to working with the embodied experience of oppression in an educational framework is because that is essentially how I understand oppression – as something we learn (and can therefore unlearn). The narratives in Part I all reference some kind of learning process: learning how to move and dress in particular ways; learning how to position our bodies in relation to other bodies; and learning how we are punished for violating implicit social norms. In each case, the participants reflected upon what they had learned in and through their bodies, and discussed how they had begun to challenge old lessons and transform them into new knowledge.

As I learned from these research participants (and from my clients and students through the years), it became clear that having a model to facilitate their learning would have supported and enriched the process. Rather than having to identify, unpack, and reframe their embodied social learning guided mostly by intuition and persistence, they could be assisted by a set of tools that would help ensure the thoroughness, integrity, and utility of their learning process.

Many cultures throughout history have offered strategies for self-reflective and embodied learning and transformation, including the martial arts, contemplative movement practices, and indigenous rituals. However, most of them require the adoption of a particular belief system, while few of them focus on the relational domain or address issues of social power. For me, addressing the somatic effects of oppression required an approach that:

1.   emphasized the interpersonal nature of oppressive social dynamics; and
2.   encouraged those using the model to bring their existing beliefs and implicit frameworks into the learning process, rather than asking them to adopt new ones.

I was able to locate a number of such approaches within the field of anti-oppressive education. Each, in its own way, incorporates a critical social perspective and a counter-hegemonic stance into the process of learning. In other words, although these approaches emerged from within Western educational theory, they work to dismantle rather than perpetuate the oppressive traditions of modern Western educational systems. In preparation for introducing the model of embodied critical learning and transformation in Part III, this chapter reviews key concepts from anti-oppressive education (including critical and engaged pedagogy), and articulates some strategies for how a learning process can consciously address issues of power, privilege, and difference.

Experience as education

> I believe that all education proceeds by the participation of the individual in the social consciousness of the [human] race.
>
> *(Dewey, 1897, p. 77)*

Educational theorist John Dewey (1897, 1916, 1933) believed that the best learning was experiential (that is, grounded in real-life experience), rather than focused on content conveyed by experts based on pre-established knowledge domains. According to Dewey, learning should be relevant to the issues of learners' lives in the context of real communities, and should foster their capacity to contribute to society in a free and productive way. Dewey's ideas, radical in their day, came to inform the field of experiential education, which views learning as a process in which learners actively create new knowledge from their own experiences.

Scholars in experiential learning (Boud, 1985; Kolb, 1984; Kolb et al., 2001; Kolb and Kolb, 2012) assert that we learn about the world and ourselves in an interactive, ongoing action/reflection cycle. As we encounter new information through our life experiences, these interactions with the world change our view of ourselves and our relationships to others. Any new learning is profoundly informed by who we are, what we already know, what our values are, and how our life experiences have influenced and affected us. From an experiential perspective, learning is a complex, holistic activity that is focused on making meaning of experience and which always occurs in the larger context of our lives.

A number of experiential learning theorists address the question of how to help learners become more adept and aware about the ways they make meaning from experience. For example, Jack Mezirow (1997) developed a comprehensive theory of how adults learn by making meaning of experience, and states that educators can assist students in transforming current perspectives through a process of becoming critically aware of how our assumptions influence the way we perceive, understand, and feel about our world. According to O'Sullivan (1999), transformative learning involves becoming more reflective and critical, being more open to the perspectives of others, and being less defensive and more accepting of new ideas.

By understanding knowledge as something we create from the data of our own lives (rather than something that is handed to us by a teacher with the expectation that we memorize and apply it), and as a process that is thereby personally transforming, it is then just a small step to appreciating that learning can also transform the collective.

Education as socially transformative

Education as a means of social justice encompasses a variety of approaches (including feminist, critical, multicultural, queer, and postcolonial perspectives) but anti-oppressive education can be broadly understood as any educational approach that aims to challenge multiple forms of oppression (Kumashiro, 2000). Despite the diversity that exists under its umbrella, the work of most anti-oppressive educators shares a few key tenets. Most approaches are premised on the belief that no pedagogy is politically neutral, and that conventional methods and structures of education often do more to perpetuate and conceal oppression than to undo it. By challenging the supposed political neutrality of the dominant pedagogical model, anti-oppressive educators argue that any curriculum that ignores oppression effectively supports the status quo. Rather, they insist that in order to prepare individuals for full and engaged citizenship in the societies in which they live, educators and learners must find ways to be attentive to issues of power, authority, and difference in the context of teaching and learning.

As a consequence, most anti-oppressive education approaches have developed a process (and a propensity) for asking difficult questions. They strive to attend to what is assumed, what is normalized, what is unnamed, and what is considered self-evident or "commonsense" (Kumashiro, 2002) about established institutional structures and social norms, and then to engage in critical inquiry around those issues that other educators might well take for granted.

Critical pedagogy

Critical pedagogy is one of the earliest and most influential forms of anti-oppressive education, and it offers a number of ideas that are important in understanding how oppression is learned and experienced through the body. Ira Shor defines critical pedagogy as:

> Habits of thought, reading, writing, and speaking which go beneath surface meaning, first impressions, dominant myths, official pronouncements, traditional clichés, received wisdom, and mere opinions, to understand the deep meaning, root causes, social context, ideology, and personal consequences of any action, event, object, process, organization, experience, text, subject matter, policy, mass media, or discourse.
>
> *(Shor, 1992, p. 129)*

The central tenets of critical pedagogy were first articulated by Brazilian educator and social activist Paulo Freire in the early 1970s. Freire (2000) believed that we create social and cultural realities (rather than viewing them as pre-existing and immutable structures) and that those social realities in turn create us. Because social systems (including unjust and oppressive systems) are constantly reproduced by the individuals within them, social transformation is everyone's responsibility. In order to create culture differently, Freire argued that we must understand the systems and mechanisms that perpetuate the status quo and then work to change them through reflection and action.

Freire uses the term "culture" in its broadest sense, to encompass all that is humanly created; this includes both the material and abstract products of human activity – from factories to ideologies (Heaney, 1995). Based on Freire's understanding of oppression as the limitation of access to the products of human activity, it follows that the key objective of critical pedagogy is to regain power over the creation and use of culture. Stemming from Freire's analysis of the role of culture in oppression, he posits the idea of a "culture of silence" which is characteristic of oppressed people; they are not heard by the dominant members of society. Those members of society who hold power and privilege sanction particular discourses, and perpetuate them through control of education, media, government, and other social institutions. This imposed silence of the oppressed may be taken by the oppressor to indicate a lack of response to their conditions of living, but Freire argued that it merely reflects a lack of critical consciousness about their situation, and the absence of avenues of communication for making their voices heard. He insisted that no matter how submerged we are in the culture of silence that surrounds oppression, we are all capable of a critical consciousness of social reality (Freire, 2000).

Critical consciousness is the ability of an individual to perceive, analyze, and evaluate those aspects of their lived experience as members of a culture in which they feel manipulated, coerced, or oppressed (Freire, 2000). Those who develop a capacity for critical consciousness become capable of analyzing the world around them in ways that make visible assumed norms and established conventions. To borrow the metaphor of fish unable to see the water in which they swim, critical consciousness is about seeing the water. This level of consciousness is characterized by depth of interpretation, openness to revision, avoiding distortion and pre-conception, and receptivity to new ideas without necessarily rejecting traditional ones.

Engaged pedagogy

Feminist and anti-racist theorist bell hooks found Freire's ideas on critical consciousness crucial to her own understanding of oppression. Her 1994 book *Teaching to Transgress* draws significantly on Freire in developing a feminist, engaged pedagogy that is relevant to multicultural contexts. The engaged pedagogy that hooks advocates is perhaps more demanding than conventional critical pedagogy, however, in that it requires teachers to be actively "committed to a process of self-actualization that promotes their own well-being if they are to teach in a manner that empowers students" (hooks, 1994, p. 15). As one of the first feminist theorists to write convincingly about the intersecting dimensions of sexism and racism (in 1981's *Ain't I a Woman*), hooks expanded the concerns of critical pedagogy (which had largely focused on class issues) to the multifaceted and intersecting dynamics of "race" and gender. She also suggests that awareness of the body is implicit in teaching from an engaged pedagogical perspective:

> I have always been acutely aware of the presence of my body in those settings that ... invite us to invest so deeply in a mind/body split ... If you want to remain, you've got ... to remember yourself ... to see yourself always as a body in a system that has not become accustomed to your ... physicality.
>
> (hooks, 1994, p. 102)

Queer and postmodern perspectives

Anti-oppressive educator Kevin Kumashiro expands critical pedagogy by infusing a postmodern perspective (that is, one that is inherently skeptical of meta-narratives of experience, including the experience of oppression) and by challenging the assumption that a "commonsense" approach to anti-oppressive education is unproblematic. He argues that "many commonsense ways of reforming education actually mask the oppressions that need to be challenged" and that "anti-oppressive education expects to be different, perhaps uncomfortable, and even controversial" (Kumashiro, 2004, p. 111).

Informed by queer theory as well as by Buddhist philosophy, Kumashiro resists the tendency toward simplification and generalization when proposing strategies for addressing oppression through educational practice, and is careful to draw attention to the many contradictions and hidden lessons it holds. Like Dewey, he notes that teaching involves both intentional and unintentional lessons, as well as a desire for and a resistance to knowledge. He further recognizes that every curriculum is only partial (that is, it teaches some things but not others) and that the process of learning always asks learners to let go of some knowledge in order to explore new perspectives.

By emphasizing the fluid, context-specific, and highly subjective nature of teaching and learning, Kumashiro makes it clear that anti-oppressive education is not a static accomplishment or achievement; rather, it is a dynamic process that requires ongoing critical reflection. He states:

> Becoming anti-oppressive teachers requires not that we first reach a certain point, or that we first revamp everything about our teaching, or that we step outside of practical and political barriers. Anti-oppressive teaching happens only when we are trying to address the partial nature of our own teaching.
>
> *(Kumashiro, 2004, pp. 106–107)*

Perhaps most significantly for our purposes here, Kumashiro attends to the hidden lessons embedded in the educational process (in Dewey's terms, the "uneducation" that occurs when students learn something we did not intend to teach; and the "miseducation" that occurs when students learn something counter to what we tried to teach). Because we are *always* communicating as teachers (even when we are not teaching), we convey important but implicit messages about the subject matter, about schooling, about other students, and about the world outside our schools. These hidden lessons emerge from our silences, behaviors, curricular structures, and institutional norms, and often have greater impact on students than the intentional ones. Kumashiro further acknowledges that every student learns something different from the same lesson (including the hidden ones), depending on their own unique perspectives, contexts, and capacities. He notes that the importance of the hidden curriculum does not suggest that anti-oppressive teaching requires us to purge these implicit lessons from our educational environment. Rather, anti-oppressive teaching asks us to question the everyday interactions we have with students (and with one another) in a way that attends to the uncertain, the paradoxical, and the invisible with respect to issues of power.

Implications for a model of embodied critical learning and transformation

The educational theories outlined above argue that education is fundamental to overcoming circumstances of entrenched social oppression. They assert that we learn through experience (including our experiences of the social world) and that through reflection and action we can change that world. However, our actions must be informed by an awareness of how societies are created and reproduced – we must be literate about the sociocultural conditions in which we live.

Both Freire (2000) and hooks (1994) have argued that literacy is a powerful instrument for social change. They regard literacy as critical for allowing those who experience being marginalized and discriminated against in society to acquire a critical consciousness of their oppression.

The fact that the field of education (both conventional and critical) is relatively silent on matters of the body should not be taken as an indicator that the body is not especially relevant to how we learn (and more specifically to how we learn oppressive social systems). Rather, Freire would likely argue that this silence merely reflects a lack of critical consciousness about the body, and the absence of avenues of communication for making its voice heard. Perhaps what is currently missing from anti-oppressive education is an approach to literacy that acknowledges the ways we learn and know through our bodies, or what Paul Linden (1994) calls "somatic literacy."

A small number of educators have begun to write about the importance of the body in the process of conventional school-based teaching and learning (Dixon and Senior, 2011; Nguyen and Larson, 2015), and despite their peripheral position within the dominant educational discourse, scholars such as Sherry Shapiro (1999) and others (Berila, 2015; Drew, 2014; Granger, 2010; Michelson, 1998; Wagner and Shahjahan, 2015; Wilcox, 2009) have begun to map out what a truly embodied critical pedagogy might look and feel like. In describing Shapiro's work, critical theorist Peter McLaren argues that "knowledge is as much about bone, gristle, and capillaries as it is about objective fact and universal values" and that

> no matter how distant, removed, and powerless human beings feel in relation to the complexity of contemporary social and economic life, they carry the mega- and microstructures of social life in the machinery of their flesh, in the pistons of their muscle, and in the steely wires of their tendons.
>
> *(McLaren's Introduction in Shapiro, 1999, p. ix)*

This assertion – that we know in our bodies what it means to live in the social world, and that we can harness this knowledge to change society – is the underlying premise upon which this book (and the model of embodied critical learning and transformation embedded within it) is founded.

What remains to be addressed is how to access, articulate, and apply this implicit knowledge, given how little most of us are taught about our embodied selves. For this task, the work of somatic theorists and practitioners is an invaluable resource. In the next chapter, I introduce some of the key figures and essential ideas of a somatic approach to learning – one that privileges the first-person, felt experience of the body in how we come to know and shape reality.

Notes

1 Intersectionality is a concept first highlighted by Kimberle Crenshaw (1991). An intersectional perspective seeks to understand how different forms of oppression interact on multiple and often simultaneous levels.
2 This conceptual framework was introduced in Chapter 1.

10

LEARNING THROUGH THE BODY

In the previous chapter, I outlined some of the educational theories that inform my approach to embodied critical learning and transformation, and suggested that one of the most resounding silences in educational theories, pedagogical practices, and institutional structures had to do with the body. Traditional schooling largely ignores the body, except to address it as a possession that must be properly maintained; that is, healthy, physically fit, and not inappropriately sexual. Accordingly, physical education and health classes currently constitute the main sources of explicit instruction on the body. Implicitly, however, we also learn in school that the body must be disciplined to sit quietly indoors for long periods of time, should adapt to being fed on schedule, and must never distract the mind from its central role in learning.

Informally – in school and outside it – we learn that bodies ought to look and move in certain ways in order to be considered normal or socially desirable. Unless/until our body falls outside prevailing social norms, we go through life being able to pay almost no attention to it. As a result, very few of us possess the kind of somatic literacy required to engage deeply and skillfully in processes of embodied relational learning and unlearning. As preparation for working with the model of embodied critical learning and transformation introduced in Part III, this chapter focuses on somatic theory and practice; that is, the conceptual foundations and practical strategies for learning through (and with) the subjective, felt experience of the body.

To begin with, a brief historical and cross-cultural overview of philosophies of the body may be useful, particularly since our understandings of the body have changed over time and differ across cultures. What these shifting perspectives underscore is that the "body" is not a static or universal entity, despite the degree to which we may have assumed that it is. In order to work with embodied experience in the context of multiple social positions and complex cross-cultural interactions, it seems crucial that facilitators of such processes recognize the fluid and contested nature of embodiment itself.

The body across cultures and times

Most ancient cultures understood their worlds mythically and holistically, and this integral perspective is reflected in their conceptions of the body/mind/environment relationship (Walker, 1988). For example, many early cosmologies across the globe employed the natural elements of earth, water, air, and fire as comprising the essential components of life, including the human body. Hippocrates, long considered the founder of Western medicine, developed a psychophysiological doctrine based on these elements in the fifth century BCE. His theory that imbalances in elementally based bodily fluids caused both physical and psychological illness was later adopted by ancient Greek, Roman, and Islamic physicians. The Indian Ayurvedic tradition also established the elemental composition of the physical environment as central to bodily and psychological healing (Godagama, 1997). Similarly, ancient Chinese philosophers continued the theme of viewing the body/mind as a unified microcosm of the larger universe, influenced by the same elemental components (Pregadio, 1996). By representing the human body as intrinsically embedded in the larger world through its elemental composition, and viewing these elements as informing both our physical and psychological constitutions, these primal perspectives understood the body/mind/environment relationship as unified aspects of a functional whole.

Body/mind unity (*shinjin ichinyo*) is also an ancient and important Buddhist philosophical concept. Despite sitting meditation and other enlightenment practices that appear to strive toward transcendence over the body, Eastern philosopher and scholar Yasuo Yuasa (1987) argues that transcending the self/ego is not the same as transcending the body. He asserts that Buddhist precepts understand the body/ mind as an evolving system that can be cultivated through practice and attention. According to Yuasa, all knowledge must be cultivated – that is, learned through the body – and the lived experience of the body/mind unity is the methodological route to enlightenment. *Satori* (enlightenment) is not conceptualized as *transcendence* over the body, but *integration* of the body/mind.

In contrast to the primal and Eastern conceptions of the body/mind, the Hellenic intellectual tradition separated body and mind, and devalued the body and its perceptions as unreliable and illusory. In a philosophical legacy extending from Plato and Socrates to Descartes, the physical senses were regarded as imperfect instruments in perceiving the objective truth of external reality; only the mind was considered capable of accurately discerning and understanding the true essence of existence. Bodily experience was actually thought to inhibit and impair our attempts to understand the nature of reality (Murphy and Murphy, 1969).

This perspective has been profoundly influential on Judeo-Christian theological traditions, as well as on later philosophical schools of thought. In many ways, Western philosophy has been dealing with the implications of the dualism posited by these Greek philosophers since it was initially proposed. While the distinction between mind and body in Western thought can be traced to the Greeks, it was the work of René Descartes that provided the first systematic account of the mind/body relationship. In his 1658 treatise *De homine*, Descartes provided an articulation of mind/body interactionism that argued that conscious sensation was an example of body affecting mind, while voluntary action came about by mind affecting body. Body and mind were conceived as separate entities, with body considered distinctly inferior – closer to animals than to humans – and its perceptions considered unreliable and illusory (Murphy and Murphy, 1969). In short, Descartes' philosophical legacy positions bodily experience as a flawed and murky lens with which to view the objective nature of reality.

Considering that Descartes was writing at the time of the Western Enlightenment, when human potential was ostensibly being rediscovered and celebrated, his emphasis on the potential of the rational, cognitive aspects of human experience was to have a lasting impact on the subsequent devaluing of the body and to govern most subsequent philosophical thought until the early twentieth century.

The phenomenological body

Phenomenology offers perhaps the most significant philosophical challenge to Cartesian dualism's approach to the body. Developed in the first half of the twentieth century by Edmund Husserl, Martin Heidegger, Maurice Merleau-Ponty, and others, phenomenology is the study of "phenomena" from a subjective perspective; that is, things and events as we experience them from a first-person point of view. Because phenomenology does not consider reality as something existing independently from the structures of consciousness that perceive that reality, it is particularly interested in the study of consciousness, and how we make meaning of experience (Sokolowski, 2000).

Merleau-Ponty's work offers an embodied, existential form of phenomenology that emphasizes the role of the body in human experience. In his *Phenomenology of Perception* (1945), he developed the concept of the body-subject and argued that consciousness, the world, and the human body are intricately intertwined and mutually engaged. For Merleau-Ponty, physical reality is not composed of the unchanging objects of the natural sciences but is a correlate of the body and its sensory functions:

> My existence as subjectivity [i.e., consciousness] is merely one with my existence as a body and with the existence of the world, and because the subject that I am, when taken concretely, is inseparable from this body and this world.
>
> *(Merleau-Ponty, 1945, p. 408)*

In essence, he argues that all consciousness is embodied (and therefore in and of the world), and the body is infused with consciousness[1] (of the world). The implication of this assertion is that one's own body is a necessary condition of experience. Merleau-Ponty's elaborations of body image and embodied intersubjectivity also provide key concepts in understanding a phenomenology of the body. The body image is the corporeal schema or map that unconsciously structures our perceptions, movements, gestures, posture, and our sense of position in relation to the environment; in short, it accounts for our way of being in and through the body. For Merleau-Ponty (1945), this body image is a work in progress; it develops through experience much in the way a photographic image gains definition and resolution as it develops.

Merleau-Ponty also asserts that becoming a body-subject depends on being with other lived bodies. His notion of intercorporeality accounts for the understanding that while my body image locates me at a central "here," I can conceive that another body has its own "here." Further, I can think of the other body as having a "here" such that my body's position is a "there" for it. Put another way, intercorporeality acknowledges that each individual lives in a multi-personal field, and that this field conversely inhabits the individual (Tanaka, 2015). Embodied experience and the relational world are so deeply intertwined that intercorporeality grounds and sustains our ability to relate to the world. By the same token, however, intercorporeality implies that we remain exposed to the other and can take the other's different perspectives on ourselves.[2] Because we are always in relation to the gaze of the other, we are open to being seen even when we are alone.

These notions of the body-subject, body image, and intercorporeality provide a compelling counterpoint to Cartesian body/mind dualism and are important for understanding how an embodied learning process might shift our experience of social reality. Put another way, if the whole body is conscious (and if consciousness is wholly embodied), and if all body experience is profoundly a relational experience, then making conscious changes in the social world requires the active participation of our bodily selves. The following section elaborates further on these ideas by introducing somatic theories that expand our conceptions of the body as subject and relational body use as modifiable and available to consciousness.

Somatic perspectives on embodiment

> People say that what we're all seeking is a meaning for life. I don't think that's what we're really seeking. I think that what we're seeking is an experience of being alive, so that our life experiences on the purely physical plane will have resonances with our own innermost being and reality, so that we actually feel the rapture of being alive.
>
> *(Campbell and Moyers, 2011, p.5)*

Existential philosopher Thomas Hanna (1988), founder of the field of somatics in the United States, defines the *soma* (after the Greek word meaning "living body") as the body as experienced from within. This definition draws its inspiration from Husserl's "somatology," a study of the relationships between direct bodily knowing and scientific knowledge about the body (Johnson, 1995). An expanded definition of *soma* might be the body/mind as experienced from within, as a somatic paradigm is essentially holistic (Greene, 1997). It understands awareness, biological function, and environment as indivisible aspects of a synergistic whole. Somatics, then, represents a significant departure from conventional ways of thinking about the body and reality. It draws upon existential, evolutionary, and phenomenological perspectives to suggest that we do more than simply perceive reality through our bodily senses; reality is constructed by the way in which we perceive it (Greene, 1997).

This reality construct requires both sensory and cognitive perception. Body and mind are not viewed as separately functioning entities, but are connected through the integrative function of perception that relates us to our environment. Therefore, somatic theory suggests that what we experience as reality depends on the quality of somatic perception we bring to our engagement with the world. Rather than detracting from the authenticity of our data, the sensory perceptions of our bodily experience are essential to any inquiry into the nature of reality, including social reality.

In the same way that our sensory and cognitive perceptions create an integrated somatic experience of our external environment, what we refer to as "body" and "mind" also work together to help weave the perceptual fabric of our internal environment. This inner world includes awareness of our internal biological functioning as well as our emotions, ideas, and imaginings. The mind is not seen as a separate system with distinct components and self-contained dynamics. Rather, it is a function, one of many facets of somatic experience, and its nature changes with the *soma* (Johnson, 1983).

Further, what are typically conceptualized as "internal" processes – perceptual awareness and biological function – are understood as integrally connected with the "external" environment. From a subjective, first-person consciousness, reality is both located in the inner realm and simultaneously connected to the external world. Or, more accurately, reality is an integrated process in which perceptions inform responses which inform environment which inform perceptions, and so on.

This idea is important to understanding how somatic experience impacts upon social reality. In Western culture, we are not accustomed to expecting changes in our social environment as a result of making changes in our bodily environment, especially when those changes may consist of only a shift in awareness, rather than overt behavior. A somatic perspective understands that a change in one aspect of our experience affects all the others. Our perceptions of the external environment affect our perceptions of the inner one. Shifts in physical musculature create adjustments in our emotional state. Changes in sensory phenomena inform changes in cognitive perceptions, which, in turn, affect our relationship to the environment. And, ultimately, our engagement with the environment both forms and informs reality.

According to Hanna (1970), a number of philosophical and theoretical perspectives are congruent with, and inform, somatic theories of embodiment. For example, German philosopher Immanuel Kant introduced the notion that external reality is not so much given to us through our senses as it is constructed by us through our perceptive faculties. Merleau-Ponty's phenomenological explorations into the nature of human consciousness emphasized the centrality of perception to consciousness, and Swiss psychologist Jean Piaget affirmed this through his studies of the reality constructs of children at various developmental stages. Søren Kierkegaard's advocacy of self-discovery through "biological introspection" and Friedrich Nietzsche's assertion that human beings are overly attuned to the environment support the somatic perspective of privileging the subjective experience of the body in order to correct a historical imbalance that marginalizes this dimension of human experience. Hanna considers these philosophical developments that support somatic experiencing to be evolutionary in nature; that is, they are part of a movement toward increased adaptability of the species to an ever-changing environment.

A somatic perspective understands one of the implications of this imbalance as a narrowing or constriction of consciousness that results in less freedom, fewer choices, and less functional patterns of embodied engagement with the environment (Hanna, 1970). It is as if those techniques of the body that were once very conscious (when we first learned them) have become dimmed by habit, lack of attention, and the passage of time. Eastern philosopher of the body Yasuo Yuasa (1987) describes this as a form of "dark consciousness" and asserts that embodiment practices that focus on regaining awareness of the felt experience of the body can illuminate these lost regions of body and make them available to the "bright consciousness" of everyday awareness. The point, of course, is not for all our daily movement patterns to be returned to the state of hyperconsciousness required to learn them in the first place, but that the qualities and consequences of those patterns should be available to us for further exploration, and possible re-patterning.

Somatic practices are designed, then, to help facilitate awareness of body use and support its modification toward a more functional integration between *soma* and environment. The next section provides a brief overview of these practices, articulates some of the goals and intentions of somatic education, and outlines some of the professional embodied knowledge of somatic educators germane to our project.

Somatic education

Somatic education can be understood from a variety of perspectives, depending on the disciplinary context within which it is viewed. Within the fields of K-12 and higher education, for example, it can rightly be considered a form of holistic education that integrates the experiential knowledge of bodily senses, perception, and mind/body interaction (Matthews, 1998). An increasing appreciation (and evidence) for the situated nature of learning and the value of tacit knowledge (Durrance, 1998; Ericsson and Simon, 1998) lends credence to an educational approach that recognizes the body as a legitimate source of knowledge. Drawing strongly on Lakoff and Johnson (1999) claim that all thought, language, and abstract conceptualization arise from our embodied experience. They argue that the subjective felt experience of the body forms an important part of the fundamental grounding for human cognition and language. Damasio (1999) describes the growing empirical evidence in support of the idea that the mind is embodied. He argues that framing cognition as a purely internal, symbolic, and abstract activity neglects to account for the learning that occurs in dynamic interplay between individual bodies and their environment.

In alignment with a significantly increased scholarship on the body and embodiment (Price and Shildrick, 1999; Weiss and Cohen, 2003), a number of academics are now writing specifically about the body in relation to the discipline of education.[3] Historically, however, much of the professional activity related to learning through the body has been taught, practiced, and researched outside mainstream educational institutions.[4] Within those contexts, somatic education can be more properly understood as a group of movement and bodywork practices that privilege the felt experience of the body. Following from somatic theory, somatic education could be defined as the disciplinary field that embraces a variety of methods concerned with the living body's subjectively experienced capacity for learning through engagement with (and within) its environment.

In her book *Discovering the Body's Wisdom*, which provides an overview of more than seventy-five embodiment practices from both Eastern and Western traditions, Mirka Knaster (1996) distinguishes between structural and functional approaches. The former work with the body to help shape changes in its structure, through direct manipulation and movement techniques. In particular, they focus on postural alignment with gravity, the skeletal system, and the myofascia.

Whereas structural approaches work with the arrangement of body parts and their relationship with one another (not unlike structural functionalist approaches to social theory), functional approaches address how the body is used rather than how it is structured.[5] They understand the body as a process of moving, acting, and reacting in relationship to itself and the environment. They are concerned with recognizing habitual tendencies, patterns, and dynamics, and regard awareness of those processes as the key to facilitating change. Because of this emphasis on awareness, most somatically oriented embodiment practices can be understood as functional, rather than structural, approaches. By creating opportunities for awareness, and bringing previously unconscious mannerisms and habits to consciousness, somatic practices offer individuals the opportunity to explore alternate choices, and develop strategies for change.

Since the 1970s, somatic education (or somatics) has become an umbrella term used in Europe and North America to refer to a variety of techniques and practices that are designed to help cultivate awareness of behaviors that impede the adaptive potential of human beings in relation to their environment (Greene, 1997). In 1988, the International Somatic Movement Education and Therapy Association (ISMETA) was founded to recognize and certify practitioners.[6] There are nearly thirty different approaches or schools under the ISMETA umbrella, including Alexander Technique, Body Mind Centering, Continuum, and Laban Movement Analysis. Beyond those formally recognized by ISMETA, there are dozens of other recognized somatic approaches and techniques around the world. Within the fields of clinical and counseling psychology, body psychotherapy and dance movement therapy also employ a somatic perspective, and each is represented by professional organizations with international scope.

Components of a somatic approach

According to Hanna (1970), a somatic perspective is one that privileges the subjective felt experience of the body in understanding and working with human experience. In other words, when making meaning of an experience, what we feel in our bodies is always incorporated into what we (or others) "think" about that experience. When working with the body, our interventions are primarily informed and guided by the impact those interventions have on our bodily sense of ourselves. But what comprises this embodied felt experience? Below I list some frequently referenced, sometimes overlapping, components.

Interoception

- Perception of internal regulation responses, including pain, pressure, temperature, itch, visceral sensations, fatigue, hunger, thirst, and "air hunger."
- There is increasing research evidence that the neural substrates responsible for subjective awareness of emotions are based on the neural representation of physiological states (Craig, 2002).
- Interoception seems to provide the basis for the subjective image of the material self as a feeling (sentient) entity (Craig, 2002).
- Many, if not most, "somatic" practices focus on the exploration and cultivation of interoception as a key aspect of embodied experience (Knaster, 1996).
- The intentional, focused, and impartial observation ("witnessing") of these inner-body sensations has been posited as the basis of many mindfulness practices (Farb et al., 2015).

Exteroception

- Perception of stimuli arising from outside the body.
- The classic five senses of sight, hearing, smell, taste, and touch.
- Recent studies in experimental psychology suggest that exteroception interacts with interoception to provide a unified sense of bodily self (Tsakiris, 2017).

Proprioception

- Perception of the relative position of neighboring parts of the body and strength of effort being employed in movement.
- In humans, it is provided by proprioceptors in skeletal muscles, tendons, and joints.
- Along with the vestibular system (the sensory system that provides a sense of balance and spatial orientation), proprioception informs our overall sense of body position, movement, and acceleration and guides somatic motor activity.

- It has been proposed that the sense of self originates from the sensitivity to spontaneous movements (Haselager et al., 2012).

Felt sense

- Eugene Gendlin (1982) defined "felt sense" as an embodied, nonverbal inner knowledge.
- This implicit form of knowing represents "a special kind of internal bodily awareness ... a body-sense of meaning" which the conscious mind is initially unable to articulate (Gendlin, 1982, p. 10).
- A felt sense is more than a sensation or an emotion, although it often has a sensory quality and an emotional tone.

Intercorporeality

- As noted earlier in this chapter, intercorporeality was first proposed by Maurice Merleau-Ponty (1945). It is now being elaborated through neuroscientific study, particularly by research into mirror neurons.
- It highlights the role of social interaction in the experience and behaviors of the body as we "try on" the experiences of others through our embodied imagination.

In somatic education, practitioners draw upon all of the components defined above to help students explore the role of the body in experience, increase their understanding of somatic phenomena and movement behavior, and incorporate the lived experience of the body into daily awareness. In effect, somatic educators help students to develop a sense of somatic literacy (Linden, 1994). In the same way that literacy can be understood as the ability to access, create, and communicate information encoded in the written word, somatic literacy is the ability to access knowledge encoded in kinesthetic and nonverbal material. This form of literacy supports authoritative knowing grounded in embodied experience. It allows us to access and use what we know in our bones. Somatic educators also strive to cultivate in students a capacity to tolerate unusual or unsettling experiences, to attend to experience without rushing to attachment or conclusions, and to cultivate kinesthetic empathy – the willingness and capacity to imagine viscerally in our own bodies what might be occurring in the body of another.

Beyond the somatic methods in themselves, however, the embodied knowledge of the somatic educator (and the knowledge that is communicated through the relationship between educator and student) is a significant element of the process (Johnson, 2011).

The embodied knowledge of the somatic educator

Although each practitioner names them differently (depending on the particular somatic approach in which they were trained), a number of deep underlying threads connect the embodied professional knowledge of somatic educators to the work they do. These themes function as practical principles – they embody the somatic practitioner's purpose in a deliberate and reflective way, and are expressive of the personal dimension of professional practical knowledge.

Although these principles may stand on theory (for example, the Gestalt Somatics concept of *contact*, or the Alexander Technique's *use of self*), they are also developed out of experience. Somatic principles are taught experientially as well as didactically, so that experience begins during the professional training of a somatic educator. As a practitioner becomes seasoned, they add to their own embodied knowledge, further refining and strengthening the ways that these practical principles inform their practice.

One of the most critical principles of most somatic work is presence: the ability to attend, observe, and listen to the client/student, the environment, and especially oneself. Although somatic educators are trained to be highly skilled observers, with the capacity to sense and perceive both particularly and globally, this attention involves more than just the senses of sight, sound, and touch; it also includes interoceptive awareness. Presence also involves a particular attitude toward all the elements of the interaction (client/student, teacher/practitioner, and environment), one that is captured well by the word "honor" (Johnson, 2011). It is often quiet, always respectful, and predicated on the ability to empathize kinesthetically. If *kinesthetic* refers to the sense that perceives bodily position, weight, or movement, and if *empathy* is defined as the identification with and understanding of another's situation, feelings, and motives, then *kinesthetic empathy* pursues that understanding physically rather than cognitively, allowing the somatic educator to cultivate compassion at the body level.

Kinesthetic empathy is usually facilitated by mirroring the student's movements, gestures, or posture until the teacher can feel in her own body what it might be like inside the student's body. It involves listening deeply with the body, then echoing back through the body what has been perceived. True presence requires more than attending to the student, however. It also requires attending to the self. Somatic education training offers a variety of techniques and strategies for attending to the self, depending on the particular school or method. Often, somatic educators facilitate attending to the self by noticing their breath. By coming back to an aspect of bodily functioning that is reflective of the current state of the autonomic nervous system and responsive to conscious direction, they can both assess and adjust their somatic experience of the moment.

While presence is always palpable in the teaching/learning relationship, it most often occurs as part of a relationship dynamic in which the teacher is attending both to herself and to the student, while the student attends primarily to themselves. Yet, sometimes, a moment occurs in which the student is able to be fully present in their own body *and* notice that the teacher is also fully present in hers. This mutual sense of conscious physical presence – of a living, breathing, feeling, moving, human being in full embodied awareness with another human being – is a striking feature of somatic education, and one that has particular implications for the model of embodied critical learning and transformation introduced later in this book. Through this relational embodied engagement, as well as the strategic use of somatic techniques for exploring the felt sense and behaviors of the body, a renewed relationship to the bodily self and (by extension) to the environment becomes possible.

Connecting somatic perspectives with critical praxis

Although somatic theories and practices are essentially holistic, and recognize the integrality of the environment and the *soma*, somatic scholars have not taken up sociocultural and political issues specifically, with a few key exceptions. Thomas Hanna's initial work on somatics, *Bodies in Revolt* (Hanna, 1970), clearly articulates his argument that the need for a return to the lived experience of the body is related to the evolution of the human species, in response to industrialization, rationalization, and the commodification of the body. One of the early developers of the field of somatic psychotherapy, Wilhelm Reich, also positioned social concerns as central to his work. He argued that social and economic problems were at the root of most neurosis, and articulated the concept of muscular armor as a way to defend against the impossible or contradictory demands of an unjust environment (Reich, 1980).

Somatic theory (Gendlin, 1982; Hanna, 1970; Johnson, 1983; Yuasa, 1987) further suggests that cultivating embodied consciousness produces/elicits an altered state of consciousness, and Hanna (1970) asserts that this shift in consciousness can serve as a locus for resistance against oppression. More specifically, many somatic practitioners (Johnson, 2011) argue that being intentionally anchored in a clear felt experience of the body in relation to other bodies is so phenomenologically different from the experience of "othering" or being "othered" that it provides a compelling counterpoint to hierarchical models of social power – a place from which to experience the world differently, even when the social structures through which that experience is shaped have not yet changed.

In the second "body story" in Part I, Pat describes this phenomenon in her narrative through her observation that feeling connected to her own body fundamentally changes her relationships to others in a positive way, and it has been her own body journey that has made issues of social justice real for her. Somatic theory (Greene, 1997) as well as social theory (Foucault, 1990; Johnson, 2001) would understand this process as having profound implications for social structures, based on the premise that social structures are created (and reproduced) through a web of interpersonal relations. When those relationships change – body by body – so, inevitably, do the structures.

Extending that process to embodied critical learning and transformation suggests that practices and processes that support the embodiment of clients/students simultaneously encourages the cultivation of more grounded and equitable relations with others. It should be specified that the embodiment cultivated through these proposed educational strategies is not reembodiment. That is, it is not conceived of as a return to some idealized, natural, or "authentic" state of connection with our corporeal selves (i.e., we used to be connected to our bodies as children, but the adult demands of modern society have forced us to disconnect). Rather, this integration of somatic experience and conscious awareness should be viewed as a cultivation of a capacity for deeper and richer forms of consciousness.

Yuasa (1987) called this "bright consciousness"; Hanna (1970) understood it as the evolution of the *soma*. They argue that conscious embodiment is new territory for us as a species, not a reclaiming of old ground. However, this does not align the project of embodiment with a modernist grand theory of progress; rather, the specificity and multiplicity of embodiment is more in alignment with a postmodern sensibility that recognizes the unique, fluid, and contingent nature of embodied experience.

By integrating these understandings with Judith Butler's concept of performativity (Butler, 1993), it is possible to suggest further implications for practice that speak to the question of how an embodied critical learning process might address the embodied effects of oppression. Simply stated, if the unequal social categories upon which oppression is predicated are culturally constructed through "regulative discourses" (including nonverbal communication norms as a form of discourse), it is the repetition of acts shaped by these discourses that maintains the appearance of a coherent identity. In short, oppression depends upon naturalized social categories of unequal power and status. The idea that identity is performative (that it is not based on inherent and characteristic differences but is constantly created through reiterative acts) has profound implications for social change. Altering those reiterative acts disrupts the very categories of identification upon which social inequity depends. Given the significance of nonverbal communication in the development of critical consciousness that has been articulated by participants in this research, it follows that a critical praxis that attends to nonverbal communication could provide clients/students with an opportunity to experiment with such changes.

In Part III, I will elaborate on how the embodied attitudes and capacities cultivated through somatic practice might support us to experience ourselves and others as sensitive, vulnerable, and mysterious architectures of flesh and bone, rather than meaty objects, machines, or abstractions. By then linking these somatic competencies to a process of experiential inquiry, it becomes possible to critically examine and transform how we occupy ourselves, take up space, and move through the social world.

Notes

1 The fairly recent discovery of neurons in the digestive tract suggest that our previous conceptualization of thinking as occurring only in the brain was inaccurate. See, for example, Gershon (1999).

2 The discovery of mirror neurons (Gallese, 2014) provides promising evidence of the neurobiological basis for intercorporeality. Data suggest that the mirror neuron system may help us to understand and empathize with other people's actions.

3 See, for example, Nguyen and Larson (2015), Forgasz (2015), Stolz (2015), Hopwood (2017), Ali-Khan (2016), and Drew (2014).

4 Although the research literature on somatic education is still relatively sparse, a number of studies identify key issues that are germane to this project. For example, Beckett and

Morris (2001) and Brockman (2001) establish the body as a legitimate source of knowledge, and argue that somatic education helps learners to become more adept in the process of constructing and deconstructing knowledge. Holst (2013) suggests that becoming more aware of the states, postures, and expressions of the body is key to integrating a sense of human embodiment into physical education, and Fortin (1998) asserts that the awareness of embodied experience provides an alternative to learning through observation, and that it encourages students to question the hegemony of established knowledge sources. By extension, cultivating access to embodied knowledge could offer a locus for questioning and resisting dominant discourse, as suggested by Wagner and Shahjahan (2015). When this is paired with an emphasis on developing the capacity for kinesthetic empathy, somatic education has the potential to support mutual respect and empowerment. In particular, the concepts of presence, engagement, somatic literacy, and kinesthetic empathy may inform how we bring our bodies to the navigation of power differentials in relationships with others. Not only do somatic educators possess skills and qualities that can support learners to access, articulate, and transform embodied experience, but Beaudoin (1999) suggests that somatic learning lends itself to integration into daily life, making the changes that occur in the educational setting transferable to social contexts.

5 Note that the ways in which Knaster uses the terms "structural" and "functional" are not analogous to the ways in which these terms are used in sociology and anthropology.

6 See www.ismeta.org, accessed March 29, 2017.

PART III

Grasping and transforming the embodied experience of oppression

11

THE CYCLE OF EMBODIED CRITICAL LEARNING AND TRANSFORMATION

As practitioners working in complex social environments, we each bring a unique perspective on issues of social justice, based on the intersecting dimensions of our own personal history and professional development. Our students and clients, of course, bring a similarly diverse set of understandings, assumptions, and practices. Whether our professional context is education, counseling, community work, or healthcare, the interactions that result from these differing perspectives can often be challenging to navigate. For many of us, staying current in terms of multicultural awareness and sensitivity training is an important first step, but content knowledge alone can be insufficient in preparing us to work skillfully with others, especially when dealing with situations where facilitating understanding through a relational process[1] may be more helpful than simply conveying knowledge about oppression.

In the previous parts of this book, I offered examples of how oppression informs (and is informed by) our bodily experience in the world, and began a process of linking the lived experiences of my research participants with key concepts in anti-oppressive and experiential education, nonverbal communication research, traumatology, and somatic theory and practice. Through this reiterative process of integration – connecting embodied experience to theory and research from the ground up – a set of implications for practice eventually emerged. Based on the findings of my research and the scholarly literature that supports it, a comprehensive and inclusive approach to social justice work would be one in which oppression is understood as learned (rather than innate) behavior, and in which the body's learning is figural. It would facilitate (un)learning that is experiential and relational, recognize the complexity of intersecting social identities, support somatic literacy and fluency in body language, and recognize the traumatic imprint of oppression on embodied experience. The model described in this chapter represents my own attempt[2] to address these multiple requirements in a format that is accessible and relevant to counselors, educators, and human services professionals working across a range of professional contexts.

Introducing the cycle

This chapter describes a model of transformative learning that privileges the knowledge of the body (e.g., bodily sensation, body image, and nonverbal communication) in exploring issues of social power, privilege, and difference. In developing it, I am significantly indebted to the work of David Kolb (1984; Kolb et al., 2001; Kolb and Kolb, 2012), whose cycle of experiential learning serves as its foundation. Readers familiar with his work will see the clear outlines of his four-stage cycle in my model, as well as the ways these phases have been elaborated and refined to address issues of embodiment and social justice more specifically.

Building on the work of Dewey and Freire (as discussed in Chapter 9), Kolb's experiential learning theory consists of a cycle with four stages:

1. experiencing (often called concrete experience);
2. reflecting (reflective observation);
3. thinking (abstract conceptualization); and
4. acting (active experimentation).

According to Kolb, these stages represent the natural process of learning from experience.[3] In other words, it is how we learn in the absence of formal instruction – intuitively reflecting, distilling, and experimenting – and we already know how to do it, albeit with varying degrees of effectiveness. We "grasp" experiences by feeling and thinking about them, and "transform" them by observing and doing. Although there are differences in which strategies people prefer, Kolb argues that these grasping and transforming processes are always at the heart of learning from experience.

Kolb further asserts that this innate and commonplace process can be enhanced by focusing intentionally on each phase to ensure that no aspects are overlooked, thereby maximizing the learning that is possible from any given experience.[4] Learners wishing to facilitate their own learning process can begin anywhere on the cycle (although the "experiencing" phase is a typical starting point), and often find that moving through one phase leads to the next, so that learning from experience is an ongoing process – one that looks more like a spiral than a cycle when mapped onto real life.

The second major influence on the development of the cycle of embodied critical learning and transformation is the work of philosopher Eugene Gendlin, who developed a six-step technique called *focusing*. Based on groundbreaking research into the effectiveness of psychotherapy at the University of Chicago in the late 1960s, *focusing* is a body-centered approach to exploring personal questions and concerns that harnesses our innate capacity to "tap into" implicit knowing. By paying attention to our inner, embodied felt sense, the *focusing* process helps to uncover insights and understandings that may otherwise elude our conscious awareness. Although Gendlin (1982) asserts that this process is a natural one (as does Kolb with respect to experiential learning), he argues that it is possible to improve our innate capacity to focus by learning and following six steps that aim to establish an interaction between our rational understanding and our somatically rooted "knowing." Briefly, these steps consist of:

1. Clearing a space by attending to the core of the body and setting an intention to focus on a particular issue, problem, or experience.
2. Getting a felt sense by allowing vague, overall impressions of the experience to emerge through the body without pressing for clarity or solutions.
3. Finding a handle; that is, allowing a word, image, or movement to emerge organically from the felt sense that captures the essence of the issue and results in a bodily felt shift of recognition, rightness, and/or relief.
4. Resonating through a process of comparing the handle with the felt sense to ensure fit.
5. Asking; or checking in with the body to see if there is anything else that needs attention.
6. Receiving; or accepting the information and expressing appreciation for the process.

Although *focusing* is a complete process in itself and can be undertaken alone, it is often incorporated into psychotherapy (Gendlin, 2012; Parker, 2014) and is frequently conducted in dyads; that is, even when only one person is *focusing*, a partner is present to facilitate the process and provide supportive witnessing. Underscoring the relational dimensions of learning and transformation, Gendlin (2005) suggests that while working with a partner is not essential to the effectiveness of *focusing*, the depth and ease of the process can be enhanced by the presence of another person. This recognition of our intercorporeal embeddedness supports the recommendations of Romney et al. (1992) and Johnson (2001) to engage the challenges of social injustice by engaging with others, rather than working alone.

As I applied Kolb's cycle of experiential learning and Gendlin's *focusing* to my own professional work as a psychotherapist, social worker, and educator, I came to appreciate the effectiveness of partnering/facilitation in working the experiential learning cycle, and how well the *focusing* steps elaborated the reflection and conceptualization phases. Eventually, I found it impossible to teach/facilitate one model without teaching/facilitating the other. Working the two processes together effectively created an embodied cycle of experiential learning, as incorporating Gendlin's *focusing* steps into Kolb's cycle immediately brought the learning into the body.

Although I found this integrated cycle of embodied learning remarkably useful in my clinical and teaching work across a range of topics and issues, it was issues of social justice that seemed to benefit most from engagement with this process. In particular, experiences of embodied microaggressions, struggles with body image, and events that provoked somatic dissociation often responded well to exploration using the cycle as a template or guide. I wondered if the implicitly embodied nature of these experiences is suited to a process that works through the body to make vague somatic sensings and apprehensions more accessible, intelligible, and actionable. Over time, I expanded my facilitation of the reflection and experimentation stages to be more inclusive of multiple perspectives and critical social analysis. I also incorporated elements from Gestalt therapy, dance movement therapy, psychodrama, and bodywork into my facilitation of each phase of the cycle to enhance their relational and somatic dimensions.

The cycle of embodied critical learning and transformation (as I have named the process I adapted from the work of Kolb, Gendlin, and others) reflects an ongoing process of tweaking and testing to incorporate the elements that my research suggested were important for working with issues of social justice.

Although the cycle appears remarkably similar to Kolb's cycle on the surface, there are a number of important distinctions and elaborations embedded within the details of each phase. In the sections below, I describe a process of consciously embodying an experience of oppression, reflecting on that experience from multiple perspectives, making meaning of that experience through the body, and then engaging with new ways of being in the body (and in the world) that are informed by the learning gleaned from the process.

The cycle of embodied critical learning and transformation can be employed in two ways. The first (and most common) is to use the cycle to unpack and resolve an experience that has already occurred, either in your own life or in the life of a client or student. For each phase of the cycle described below, I provide an illustration of that phase drawn from the experience of someone using the cycle to learn more about their own embodied experience of oppression.

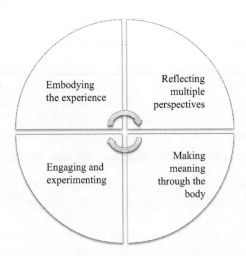

FIGURE 11.1 Cycle of embodied critical learning and transformation

The second way I use the cycle is as the framework for designing and facilitating experiential exercises focused on the topic of oppression. Given that this book is written for professionals who will be curious about how they might apply this model to their own practice, I also elaborate the model from my perspective as a facilitator. An illustration of this facilitated cycle is included at the end of the descriptions.

Phase one: embodying the experience

This phase of the cycle of embodied critical learning and transformation focuses specifically on recalled (or elicited) experiences of privilege, discrimination, or marginalization, and deliberately includes somatic data and nonverbal behavior. Like Kolb's cycle, the cycle of embodied critical learning and transformation usually starts with a concrete experience – a real-life occurrence or event of some kind. Although many kinds of recalled experiences can be worked with, one of the first challenges I encounter when I use this cycle with clients or students is helping them identify and choose a suitable experience. Part of this challenge lies with the fact that our life experiences rarely parcel themselves neatly into discrete chunks, with a clear beginning, middle, and end. Experiences are often complex and messy, with several narrative threads, multiple characters, and compelling background storylines. That said, I have found that single, brief encounters work better than an extended series of events, and that events in which the body already figures strongly in the story are easier to work with than experiences in which the somatic elements are submerged within the experience.

The following excerpt is from a paper written by a student in one of my graduate courses on embodied social justice (used here with their permission). It illustrates a good choice of experiences to work with and exemplifies how describing the experience as if it were occurring in the present helps to bring it back to life so that it can be more fully explored:

> I'm standing in the center of a circle of people from my Gestalt therapy class. The class is being held in the addition our instructor had built on her home for the purpose of holding group therapy. It has a view of the mountains. We're standing on an expensive wool Persian rug and sunlight filters in the French doors and over her geraniums, rosemary, and ivy, potted and placed around the room. My classmates are waiting while I try to think of something that I am "more than" or "less than" as part of a diversity exercise. When I say something, everyone who is like me is supposed to move from their spot while I try to grab a free spot and get out of the circle. I feel my shoulders tense as my mind races for something to say. I crane my neck to look at the list we've created – behind it is her backyard and expansive garden. We're supposed to "take a risk" which feels to me more like we are playing "truth or dare" than anything designed to foster awareness. This reminds me of the awkwardness of being a teenager and not knowing quite how my legs should

hold up my body – too far apart was wrong, I somehow knew. Below my neck, my body feels numb. I imagine I can feel the eyes of my classmates on me and I imagine they are waiting for me – the queer one, the smart one, the one with the most to risk – to reveal something that they will all identify or not identify with.

As you can see from this example, the author has set a context that includes a rich description of the physical and social environments. They have also described the embodied aspects of the experience – the spatial relationship of the bodies in the room, the implied bodily movement of the exercise in which they are engaged, and the internal somatic experience of tension and numbness. They continue:

I decide on something that is a bit risky, doesn't feel like a concession to me, and which others would be able to get. I say, "I've been criticized for a non-normative gender presentation." They look at me blankly. I know they want to connect, they are thinking hard about it. No one moves. My heart jumps a little and my face flushes. "No one?" I say. They look apologetic but no one steps out. My eyes prick with tears. I feel enormous, monstrous, as if my body takes up much too much room. Fire rushes up my spine and causes a prickling – it's fury. I can't remember what finally got me out of the circle.

Here, the embodied and relational dimensions of the experience are highlighted as a central part of the narrative. When I facilitate the elaboration of embodied experience with an individual, I will ask questions designed to elicit some of the same features evident in the description above:

- Where was your body in relation to other bodies?
- What movements, gestures, and facial expressions occurred (including micro-movements)?[5]
- What sensations were present in your body?
- How were you reading the bodies of others?
- How did others appear to be reading your body?

In this example, the reader can easily identify the interoceptive sensations of distress (fire rushing up the spine, heart jumping, face flushing) and connect them with the social exclusion and invalidation being described.

Another way to begin working with the cycle is to design a somatic experiment – an experiential exercise intended to elicit an embodied experience – rather than just asking the client/student/participant to recall an experience they have already had. These embodied experiential exercises are intended to evoke a tolerable amount of bodily sensation in relation to issues of power, privilege, and difference. Rather than design experiments that replicate oppressive interactions, however, I focus only on related topics. For example, interactive exercises on embodied boundaries, safe touch, and kinesthetic empathy can be used to highlight elements of nonverbal communication, while an exercise on "reading" bodies (using my own body as the example) helps participants explore the degree to which judgements, assumptions, and projections are based on body image. I also include experiential components designed to help participants explore how their bodies can be sites of strength, empowerment, and resistance, not just sites of distress and limitation.

These in-the-moment embodied experiences can be remarkably potent, so I am particularly careful to ensure that participants are well resourced[6] and have engaged in a thorough process of informed consent. I usually sequence the exercises along a continuum from less to more interactive, and from less to more challenging in terms of topic. They work best when I take the time to set up the experience clearly and carefully, and then allow participants to engage with it in their own way. As much as possible, I use language that is inclusive or evocative of embodied sensation or movement – for example, "As you move toward your partner, notice the quality of your breathing." I have learned not to make the experiential exercises too long or too elaborate, and to allow time for participants to transition into (and out of) a more embodied state of consciousness. In choosing or designing these experiential components, the essential criteria are that the experiences address issues of social power, and that they engage participants' bodies in some way.

Phase two: reflecting multiple perspectives

> For individuals who experience monetary, time or bandwidth poverty, reflection is a luxury good.
>
> *(Konnikova, 2014, p. SR1)*

Reflection is perhaps one of the most important aspects of the embodied critical learning process. In it, we begin the crucial task of unpacking, deconstructing, and examining each facet of an event that may initially be experienced as a chaotic or undifferentiated mass. Reflection can be done alone, in pairs, or in groups, but most people seem to need a relatively quiet and time-spacious environment to get the most from this phase of learning. Facilitating embodied critical reflection can be challenging, but asking generative, open-ended questions and guiding conversations in strategic ways can help open participants to powerful and empowering insights. As the above quote suggests, the simple act of providing time to reflect on their experiences can help support individuals dealing with oppression and discrimination. We all know what it's like to operate in crisis mode, putting out one fire after the next without a moment to investigate the cause of the flames. Reflection can be the first step in shifting out of crisis mode and into a more responsive and proactive stance.

In our continuing example, my student begins to reflect on their experience:

> In the process after the exercise, I said that I felt profoundly lonely when no one stepped out. Those that knew me expressed that they felt moved by my

experience and had empathy. By this time, I couldn't stop crying. It was as though someone had pricked me with a pin, and the tears finally had a way out. They thought I was crying because there was no one like me. This was partially true, but mostly I was crying because no one could connect with me. Every person in that room had some experience of being criticized. It wasn't that they were never criticized, it was that they never understood it as criticism or as related to their gender.

In this passage, the student begins to tease apart their embodied experience and the reactions of others, questioning their classmates' assumptions about gender identity and their implicit designation of my student as the identified other. The student continues to reflect in the passage below by asking questions and framing their observations in terms that take ownership of them; that is, "I read," "I wonder," and "I felt," rather than "They are" or "This is."

I read their empathy and reaching out not just as unmediated compassion (although some of it was, I'm sure) but also as a construction of me as a "failed woman" and "failed man." I wonder about the relationship to this in my body. Would they be responding in the same way if they felt I was a "successful" man? If they perceived me to be fully transitioned? If I had passed as a man until that moment, would they have different questions and concerns? I felt their gaze on my body as wanting it for their own purposes – to scaffold their sense of masculinity or femininity or as the weapon with which we will finally break down gender oppression. No matter that I would be a casualty of this war. I want my body back. This was what my tears mourned. My tears were not because I was understood by no one; they were not because I was alone in the world; they were because there are a lot of people who understand me and who are just as proud of who they are as I am of myself. However, they were not in that room. My tears were because that room thought I was alone and indescribable and that is profoundly insulting. I wanted to shout, "It is you who doesn't understand, you who, acted upon by ideas of gender normativity, cannot connect with anyone not like you. It is not me who is indescribable."

As you can see from this excerpt, my student is surfacing a perspective on their experience that critiques the dominant narrative on gender. Through this reflective process, they articulate gender normativity not as a problem for those whose gender expression deviates from the norm but as inherently dehumanizing for those who unconsciously conform to it.

While most experiential learning models encourage learners to examine their experiences from multiple perspectives, in this model social critique is emphasized. The dominant or default social lens is identified and a counter-hegemonic perspective is explored, as the above example clearly illustrates. As a facilitator, I actively inquire about power and privilege, and encourage participants to question social norms and assumptions. My questions are intended to illuminate all facets of an experience and evoke a tolerable amount of somatic disequilibrium; that is, embodied critical reflection can introduce feelings and perspectives that are temporarily distressing and disorienting. Embodied learning asks us to question how we hold and orient our bodily selves in relation to the world, and these shifts are not always comfortable or easy.

An attitude of inquiry and curiosity – one that suspends judgement but does not neutralize values – is crucial here. I encourage clients and students to ask themselves what is silent and what is assumed, to get curious about what questions are not being asked, and to de-center what is dominant to see what happens. When reflection is undertaken in pairs or small groups, I attend to the interactive/relational element of reflection, and support participants to privilege their own reflections over outside observations; in other words, to claim expertise on their own experience of oppression without disregarding the input of others.

In this model, participants are also asked to explore their experience from a somatic perspective. During the reflection phase, they are encouraged to be curious about how they felt in their bodies during (and after) the event, to identify the nonverbal behavior that occurred, and to use their capacity for bodily sensation and imagery to illuminate their experience. In other words, this model recognizes that reflection is not simply a cognitive process, but also occurs through bodily sensation and expression. During embodied critical reflection, participants gather an embodied "felt sense" of the experience that begins to help clarify all its possible meanings. This felt sense draws from *focusing* practice, and refers to a process of gently inquiring into all of the elements that stand between the experience and feeling good in one's body. These elements are identified and acknowledged but not plunged into; rather, they are held with attentive care until meaning can be made, as one might hold the pieces of a jigsaw puzzle until an overall pattern can be discerned.

One of the remarkable features of embodied reflection is that many of these elements, and the multiple perspectives we are seeking, are palpable within the body. Emotions, memories, values, outside demands, internal expectations, environmental conditions, and social norms almost always have a perceptible bodily dimension. For example, integrity might be experienced as a warmth in the heart or a lengthening of the spine; internalized social norms might manifest as immobilized muscles or a lump in the gut. Encouraging learners to ask themselves where these features of the experience live in their bodies can give voice to hidden dimensions and suggest new pathways for change.

When teasing apart the multiple aspects of and perspectives on an embodied experience (particularly when some of the perspectives are in apparent conflict with one another), it can sometimes be helpful to ask learners to embody one perspective at a time, rather than trying to hold them all at once. I will sometimes suggest that a client/student take time to enact a particular perspective as if they were taking on a role or character, drawing on the tools I have learned through psychodrama and Gestalt therapy. This bodily enactment of internalized messages can help them to clarify a polarized position or inner ambivalence. For example, a client/student might take on the posture and gestures of an inner aspect of self who represents the critical voices of social norms.

To summarize, the process of reflecting multiple perspectives through embodied critical reflection:

- privileges interoceptive data and nonverbal behavior;
- gathers an embodied "felt sense" of the experience;
- actively inquires about power and privilege;
- questions social norms and assumptions;
- acknowledges multiple perspectives; and
- is intended to evoke a tolerable amount of disequilibrium in the process of deconstructing an old somatic pattern or shape.

This patient process of listening to one's body (and to the bodies of others) gathers the somatic data that are so necessary for understanding how particular experiences of oppression inform, and are informed by, the body.

Phase three: making meaning through the body

After identifying, critically examining, and gathering together all the elements of an experience, the next step in the cycle asks participants to distill these various aspects and perspectives into a more cohesive and meaningful whole. In Kolb's model of experiential learning, this is referred to as the abstract conceptualization phase, and is characterized by an emphasis on thinking and hypothesizing (Kolb, 1984). In contrast, the cycle of embodied critical learning and transformation recognizes that making meaning from experience is not always a rational process, and it under- scores the role of the body in generating concepts and testing them for "fit." Here, the *focusing* method provides an excellent illustration of how the body can generate explicit knowing from implicit data. In it, the "felt shift" described by Gendlin (1982) is a bodily change and sense of release that accompanies a new under- standing of something that was previously unclear, in a process of organizing information at a higher level of integration. For example, a client/student might generate meaning from an experience in the form of a bodily sensation or image instead of a thought or cognitive concept.

When I facilitate meaning-making through the body, I often simply ask the client/student to be patiently present with all they have gathered through their reflection process, and ask them to inquire of their body, "What is this whole thing about?" I then encourage them to wait until a word, image, sensation, or gesture emerges organically from their bodily core, without actively constructing or imposing meaning. This is a "bottom-up" process that engages a bodily way of knowing that is much different from "top-down" cognitive analysis.[7] For example, a client/student making meaning of their experience of feeling judged because of their gender presentation might wordlessly distill that experience into a sensation of collapse in their ribcage. Although it might seem like this collapsing feeling is "just" a bodily sensation that accompanies the experience of feeling judged, because of the extensive reflection process they have undergone that sensation now symbolizes a whole set of understandings that has become anchored in their body. Following the basic steps of *focusing*, I would then check with them to see if the sensation of ribcage collapse "fits" with their experience of feeling judged around their body image. If they describe a corresponding affirmation on a body level (that is, a sense of release and/or relief when checking for fit), I suggest they sit with the meaning they have made until it really settles and feels right in their body. Once confirmed, this distilled sensation of collapse might lead them to ask what their body needs now, and to experiment with how they might want to shift or change that sensation (and possibly, by extension, their next experience of feeling judged around body image).

Once the client/student has made their own meaning, I sometimes offer a reference to preexisting concepts and research findings that might affirm or extend their developing understanding. For example, I might support their integrated distillation of "ribcage collapse" by offering ideas about musculoskeletal responses to chronic trauma (Scaer, 2014), or about shame and queer body image (Atkins, 1998). In this way, I help the learner stay anchored in self-generated meaning about their experience while simultaneously encouraging them to benefit from the validation and elaboration of externally generated concepts.

When I teach this process in the context of graduate coursework, the externally generated concepts often come first, in the form of assigned course readings. In our continuing example, my student draws on the readings to help support their emergent personal understanding of genderqueer identities:

> Eliot and Roen's discussion of coming to have a body through our own desire is the first time I have read a theory of personal desire included in a discussion of gender and transgender issues (Eliot and Roen, 1998). It answers Cromwell's tongue-in-cheek question: "If I have the wrong body, whose body do I have and where is my body?" I am not in the wrong body. The body I have is mine – I can love or loathe it, I can change it or dress it differently, but in the end my representation of myself is a way I can leap out of the self-injurious discussion of whether I "should" be more masculine, transition, whether I "should" stay as I am because it is more radical, whether I "should" make myself more understandable or let others struggle. The "should" is a part of it, but cannot be all of it. This is what Clare (2001) named "very internal" and which Eliot and Roen's interviewees discuss as "how I feel deep inside" and "the way I *feel* I want to behave" or as "'having feelings ... of what we'd term as a man' but having been 'born a female and ... brought up as a girl'" (Eliot and Roen, 1998, pp. 250, 256). There is a part of us that, no matter how our bodies are socially mediated, or how they are biologically determined, has a unique and powerful way of choosing representation. These representations cannot exist outside cultural pressures, but neither are they completely dictated by them.

As this example illustrates, the student's embodied knowing is enhanced by the knowledge of others, and what was initially a more internal, subjective process now connects to the larger world through the skillful and insightful integration of the scholarly literature. The connection to meanings outside oneself does not require reading theory, however. For many people, the most heartening and affirming shared meanings between self and other occur in the context of conversations with classmates and community members. Creating space for these conversations is an important part of facilitating this phase of the cycle of embodied critical learning and transformation.

To sum up, the embodied meaning-making phase of the cycle involves:

- the continuing deconstruction and problematization of experience through meaning-making that includes somatic and social data;
- generating critical insights that are embodied as well as cognitive, and that may initially take the form of embodied image, posture, or movement rather than words;
- privileging self-generated over other-generated concepts;
- naming the unnamed and unnameable; and
- an embodied "felt shift" toward a new somatic shape or pattern.

Once the embodied experience of oppression has been meaningfully explored, participants move to the task of experimenting to transform that experience in their bodies and in the world.

Phase four: engaging and experimenting

This phase of the cycle focuses on new ways of acting in (not just thinking about) the world. Specifically, it asks clients/students to experiment with solutions to the problem of embodied oppression they have identified in the previous phases of the cycle. As I ask learners to be curious about the broader implications of their experience, I also acknowledge the very real challenges and risks of enacting certain new behaviors (particularly those that transgress dominant social norms of embodiment) and the multiple social constraints on choice of action. Depending upon the social location of the learner, there may be a profound lack of systemic support for change and very limited access to resources. In those cases, an environmental audit to assess the risk of change is in order before proceeding with real-life, embodied experimentation out in the world.[8]

Before these real-life experiments occur, being able to test-run options in a relatively safe and supportive space can be remarkably useful. As a facilitator, I find it helpful to remind learners to stay connected to their embodied experience as they play with new behaviors. I also suggest that they refer back to the integrated distillation of meaning in the previous phase to assess if their embodied experiments help to shift it. For instance, the learner who noticed a sensation of collapse in their ribcage (in response to judgement about their gender presentation) might experiment with an expansion of their ribcage. To be clear, it is not that lifting their ribcage is a *solution to the problem* of feeling judged around genderqueer body image, but that lifting their ribcage will *change their experience* the next time they are in a similar situation. The shift in their body may lead to other changes (for example, feeling connected to themselves instead of disconnected from others, or feeling pride instead of shame). The process of consciously shifting an embodied shape or pattern through patient and mindful experimentation creates a ripple effect through the entire system. As Merleau-Ponty, Damasio, and Hanna remind us, our bodies and minds are functional aspects of the same whole that are always inextricably embedded in physical and relational environments.

Working this phase is well suited to a small group format, so that peer learners can help each other identify what needs to be changed, and how. Thoughtfully designed role-play exercises can provide participants with an opportunity to apply their embodied concepts to real-world contexts, and to practice new ways of being in their bodies in a relatively safe and supportive environment. The results of a learner's experiments send them into a new round of the cycle, based on this new experience of being in their body. Depending on how their experiment works, they may go back into the reflection and meaning-making phases to adjust their understanding of the issue, or develop refinements of action. Each encounter changes them, orients them to the problem or issue in a slightly (or hugely) different way. Being intentional about embodied critical reflection, embodied meaning-making, and engaged experimentation allows them to continue learning in a proactive way.

The learning that emerged for the student whose experience has served as an example through each of the phases is evident in the passage below. In it, they articulate not just a new understanding of gender but a new way to create and express it:

> This construction of identity is not something I did by myself. By connecting with one another and accepting a multitude of ways to "be a man," we are saying that it is not necessary to claim every aspect of masculinity in order to represent yourself as a man. Being a man is not a list of attributes. There can be a new way to represent masculinity that isn't about being as "real" as possible. There is language and a way to treat one another in this community that shows how we can step outside of a dichotomy. By creating an identity in contact with what I want for myself, I am not pretending to form an identity unmediated by culture or in rebellion against it, but am undermining the categories that are falsely reified and fixed. This is choosing, with awareness, integration, and power, something that fits, makes sense, and is sane and healthy.

Although the body is not made explicit in this passage, the bodily implications for the creation of a gender identity outside the dichotomy of male and female are easily imagined in this passage. Next steps have been identified and the path has been lit by the insights of self and others. Engagement, experimentation, and a future orientation are all evident here, illustrating the key features of this phase of the cycle.

In terms of facilitation, this final phase of the cycle of embodied critical learning and transformation should also attend to closure, acknowledgement, and the celebration of learning. Although engaging with one complete turn through the cycle usually leaves clients/students with a sense of completion and orientation, as a facilitator, I always think about how to build in the space and time for all learners to shift safely out of deeply interoceptive or emotionally charged states before they leave the class or session. I usually end each session with an opportunity for participants to share what was learned, and to identify the next steps in their process.

The engaging and experimenting phase of the cycle:

- tests a new shape or pattern;
- develops action plans that include interoceptive shifts and/or nonverbal behavioral changes that often challenge the sociocultural status quo;
- recognizes the social and political forces opposing change; and
- results in bodily changes and a new orientation to experience.

Embodied critical pedagogy and facilitator preparation

A hallmark of most experiential education, social work, and counseling models is the insistence that practitioners wishing to facilitate a process for someone else must prepare by thoughtfully and honestly examining our own experience with respect to the issues being addressed. In working with this model, I have found it essential to have a solid personal understanding of embodiment and oppression. This is not to suggest that, as a facilitator, I must have identical experiences to those of my clients/students (for example, personally experience homophobic discrimination) in order to be informed and helpful. It does mean that I should enter the facilitation with some awareness of my own potential triggers, blind spots, expectations, assumptions, and projections. Prior training in somatics and social justice work has also been an important prerequisite, so that I have more than my own experience to reference when facilitating someone else's.

As a facilitator, I approach this work from a perspective that acknowledges issues of power and privilege. A "top-down" instructional or counseling style is incongruent with this model, as it would serve only to reinforce preexisting asymmetries in role power between facilitator and client/student. Approaches to working with others that have emerged from liberation psychology (Martín-Baró et al., 1994), community psychology (Nelson and Prilleltensky, 2005), and feminist therapy (Burstow, 1992) offer facilitation strategies that are better suited to this model.

In the spirit of these counter-hegemonic approaches, I believe it is important to treat the learners as central to the process. My role is not to impart knowledge or information, but to help prepare learners to become actively engaged in understanding and working with their own experiences. As a facilitator, my focus should

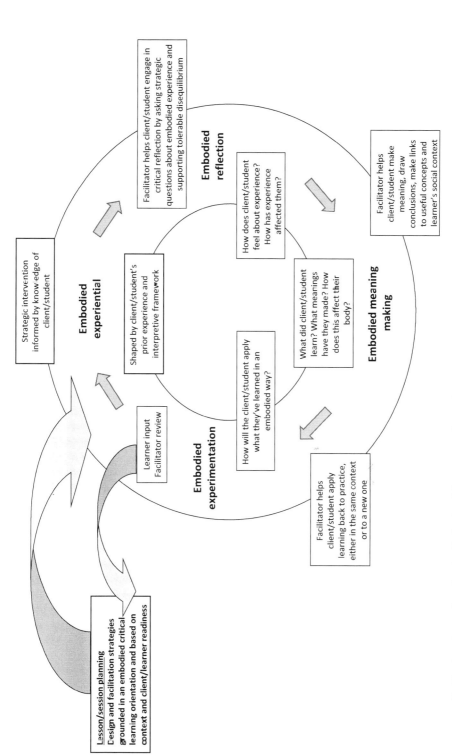

FIGURE 11.2 Facilitating the cycle of embodied critical learning and transformation

be on recognizing opportunities for learning as they occur within the field, creating an atmosphere that is conducive to honest and respectful disclosure, and supporting the critical and constructive review of an experience. I try to keep in mind that everyone learns differently, and that reactions to my facilitation and to the experiential exercises will vary across learners.

Given the often charged material being explored, I also prepare for unanticipated responses to material, and encourage multiple perspectives on a single "shared" event. I do my best to appreciate that learning and unlearning can be hard, and work to cultivate an environment where encouragement and empathy precede challenge and risk. I try to recognize my power as the facilitator, and to notice how my body communicates my beliefs, attitudes, and values to participants. To that end, I encourage participants to question my authority within the agreed norms of safety and mutual respect.

Perhaps more than is usually the case for experiential learning situations, I also attend to the setting as part of my facilitation. Although concerns such as comfortable seats, natural light, and fresh air might seem like relatively insignificant details, research shows that we are more affected by our environment that we realize (Gladwell, 2007). I have found that creating a container that supports the sensory needs of the body signals to participants that their embodied experience is valued by the facilitator.

Session/lesson planning using the cycle of embodied critical transformation

When generating ideas for exploring embodied experiences of oppression using this model, I have found it important to base my strategies on the learning/counseling context and on student/client characteristics, and to think through the objectives for any particular "exercise" or "intervention" to make sure they align with the stated objectives of the course or session. Since not everyone is familiar with an experiential approach, I take care to orient students/clients to one another and the learning/counseling context, and to engage in a process of informed consent before participants agree to take the risks entailed in opening up to experience. My orientation always includes a discussion of safety guidelines (such as confidentiality, non-coercion, and bracketing strategies), voluntary participation, and guidelines for the safe use of touch and movement.

Because I use this cycle primarily in the context of graduate coursework, I also orient participants by providing advance readings. I often assign Eli Clare's "Stolen Bodies" (Clare, 2001), which advocates for a return to the body in working with issues of gender and disability, and my own research papers on the embodied experience of oppression (Johnson, 2009, 2015), which outline the conceptual framework and research findings that are the basis for the approach.

As participants arrive and the class begins, I continue the orientation and containment process through a series of strategies and actions. I will often put a relevant, inspirational quote on the projector screen for participants to read and mull over as they arrive. As we begin, I facilitate introductions that usually include an expression of participants' hopes and fears about the course, and a body gesture that expresses how they are feeling in their bodies at that moment. From there, I provide a brief description of the course and describe the cycle of embodied critical transformation, referencing Kolb's experiential learning theory. The session then begins in earnest, with our first experiential exercise and use of the full cycle.[9]

Assessing the learning

The cycle of embodied critical learning and transformation described on the preceding pages is designed to help participants grasp and transform the experience of oppression in their bodies. As a facilitator, I believe it is important to know if this happened, and to understand what elements of the program design and session facilitation supported or hindered that process. Although practitioners working outside formal agency and institutional settings may not consider assessment an essential part of their facilitation, making evaluative mechanisms explicit and intentional can be helpful, even in individual counseling. Having clear assessment strategies helps us to understand what kind of learning (and change) is really taking place, and supports and directs our efforts as facilitators.

Program evaluation can be structured on the same cycle pattern as the model of embodied critical learning, using the same four phases:

- First, I gather participant feedback about the *experience*, both during and after the session. I ask what worked and what didn't work, and often focus specifically on embodied sensation and meaning-making, as I have learned from numerous previous evaluations that this is where participants often struggle.
- I then *reflect* on this information, and add it to my own impressions.
- I *distill* these reflections into broad themes that "feel right"[10] in my body when I consider their meaning.
- Using these themes, I revise the program or my facilitation strategies accordingly, and *experiment* with them the next time I facilitate.

Over the years, these evaluative strategies have had a significant impact on the structure, content, and delivery of the cycle. I have also come to understand the aspects of this cycle that are most valued by those who engage with it. Consistently, participants express feeling validated by a process that recognizes how much of oppression is enacted through the body. They are often relieved to realize that they are not "overreacting" when they are sensitive to embodied microaggressions or struggle with body image. Participant feedback has also underscored how important it is to cultivate the living body as a resource for personal resiliency and social advocacy. In the same way that somatic trauma models (Levine, 1997; Ogden et al., 2006) emphasize resourcing before repair, participants remark on how important it feels to engage in social justice work that feels strengthening and grounding (rather than discouraging or shaming).

Additional considerations for practitioners

Although the model of embodied critical learning and transformation described on the preceding pages is intended to be accessible to a wide range of professionals, not everyone will feel comfortable using it straight out of the box. Some practitioners will not feel at ease facilitating processes that engage and activate the body without having specialized training in somatic work, while others might hesitate to take on the work of unpacking oppression in the context of their professional roles and duties.

Taking these concerns into account, it is still possible to incorporate some relatively accessible strategies that do not require special training in somatic education or social justice. In particular, it is easily possible to become more attuned to the ways in which the use of space, gesture, and other body cues serve to communicate implicit information about social power relationships within the clinical or learning environment. The list below provides some simple suggestions of the ways in which counselors, educators, and human service professionals might make embodied social justice more explicit in their work.

- Notice the gestures, movements and facial expressions that you habitually use in various professional situations. For example, note your nonverbal communication while leading a group, while conversing with an individual client/student, and when sitting at your desk. What do you imagine you might be communicating about your integrity, authority, and approachability? Does your body support or undermine your verbal messages?
- Notice how you use space in your interactions with clients/students (and other professionals). How do others respond to your navigation of interpersonal space? How have you arranged your office/classroom? Where is your chair/desk? Where are the clients/students' chairs and desks? What do these arrangements suggest about your perspective on issues of authority, collaboration, or equality? How do these arrangements serve different types of learners?
- How do you deal with touch in the clinic/classroom? Are there spoken or unspoken rules about appropriate touch? How might the asymmetrical use of touch reinforce status and power relations?
- Observe the nonverbal communications of your clients/students. Are there differences across culture, gender, or other factors? Are there individual, personal styles or patterns? How might you work with this diversity of nonverbal communication?
- Recognize that working with the experience of the body may be relatively unknown territory for clients/students, and expect them to be correspondingly uncertain or anxious about exploring body issues. Consider ways in which you might teach clients/students body-based strategies for grounding and calming.
- Acknowledge that cultural views of the body differ, and that clients/students may hold cultural or religious beliefs about the body that make a straightforward exploration of embodied experience problematic for them.

- Attend to the power dynamics in group settings, especially with respect to how those dynamics are being created through nonverbal behavior. Consider ways in which you might provide an embodied model of conflict resolution[11] or group process.[12]

In considering ways practitioners might make their own work more inclusive of the body, the work of bell hooks is also instructive. Speaking in the context of education, she encourages teachers to be actively "committed to a process of self-actualization that promotes their own well-being if they are to teach in a manner that empowers students" (hooks, 1994, p. 15). This perspective suggests that we begin with their own bodies in the process of making our work more critically embodied.

Lastly, it is important to recognize the complexity inherent in embodied experience (as well as in issues of oppression), and to acknowledge that no model, process, technique, or theory will be universally effective, applicable, or appropriate. In that spirit, Kumashiro (2002) urges practitioners to resist the tendency toward simplification and generalization when proposing strategies for addressing oppression through educational practice, and to recognize that every curriculum (even an embodied critical one) is always partial. I would extend that caution to all models currently in use in the fields of counseling, social work, and healthcare, and to this model of embodied critical learning and transformation. The map is not the territory, and we must never privilege the map over the lived experience of our clients and students as we walk alongside them in their journey toward wholeness, integrity, and freedom.

Notes

1 On the importance of a relational strategy in anti-oppression work, see Romney et al. (1992).
2 The cycle of embodied critical learning and transformation was first published in an article entitled "Grasping and Transforming the Embodied Experience of Oppression" in the *International Journal of Body Psychotherapy* (Johnson, 2015). See Chapter 13 for links to other models.
3 Although the stages in learning from experience appear to be similar across cultures, research suggests that there are significant cultural differences in learning styles; that is, which phases of the cycle tend to be preferred or emphasized (Joy and Kolb, 2009).
4 See, for example, Kolb et al. (2001).
5 See, for example, Caldwell's work on micromovements (Caldwell, in press).
6 I discuss resourcing in more detail in Chapter 12.
7 See Levine (1997) and Ogden et al. (2006) for somatic trauma models that also apply this neuroscientific concept.
8 Sometimes the most powerful experiment is to ask for/insist upon more support.
9 Although the description in this chapter focuses on the use of this cycle with a group in a course or workshop setting, I have also used it with clients in individual counseling, and found it easily adaptable to that setting.
10 Again, I use *focusing* to help guide me to what feels right by waiting for a bodily felt shift to indicate that I have understood my experience in a way that is inclusive of implicit material.
11 See, for example, Linden (2015).
12 Claire Schmais's insights into the embodied aspects of group process are instructive here (Schmais, 1985).

12

IMPLICATIONS AND APPLICATIONS

The previous chapter outlined a model of embodied critical learning and transformation designed to facilitate the identification, exploration, and resolution of embodied experiences of oppression. Although one of the most obvious applications of the cycle is to illuminate problematic interpersonal interactions in which the individual client/student has been harmed by a misuse of social power, this should by no means be the only or most common application. For instance, a model that only addresses injuries after they have been inflicted but does nothing to support resistance and prevention subtly emphasizes reactivity rather than agency and proactivity.

Likewise, a model that cannot help us understand the harm inflicted through ignorance of our social privilege implies that the responsibility for enacting social justice lies mostly with the oppressed. In other words, for a model of embodied social justice to function as a tool of resistance and change, it must be applicable beyond "healing" the relational wounds of oppression. In this chapter, I discuss some of these applications, including ways to identify and own embodied privilege, and strategies for reclaiming body image. Although the discussion of these applications follows the main description of the cycle, they are not afterthoughts but essential elaborations.

This chapter also addresses the critical issue of body-based resilience. Many of us in the human services professions recognize the long-term nature of social justice work; we understand that change is often slow to happen and we tend to frame our efforts as a marathon rather than a sprint. As a result, it is often necessary to incorporate ongoing strategies that allow us (and our clients and students) to recharge our batteries, reconnect to our vision, and access our resources. Although these strategies are frequently framed as "self-care," that term suggests that we are somehow responsible for the depletion of our energies in working for collective human rights, and should therefore also be left to take care of ourselves when that work exhausts or injures us. Although the term "resilience" can also be problematic[1] – for instance, when it is used to suggest that failure to recover from traumatic events should be ascribed to individual weakness rather than lack of prevention and support – it does suggest that we are often (but not always) bigger than what happens to us, and that we can build muscle from adversity.

Identifying and owning embodied privilege

The research upon which this book is based did not specifically address the ways in which power and privilege are embodied, and this absence in the study is reflective of a current shortfall in the literature (Pease, 2010), although this is beginning to change. In addition to Pease's work on undoing privilege, two notable exceptions include Peggy McIntosh's ground-breaking work on white privilege (McIntosh, 1999) and Allan Johnson's contribution to the literature on power, privilege, and difference (Johnson, 2001). Working as an educator in women's studies, McIntosh attempts to understand many men's incapacity to appreciate the degree of privilege they take for granted in their interactions with women. By making extensions to her own relative unconsciousness of the privilege she holds by virtue of being white, she is able to begin to "unpack" and take some personal ownership over the amount of power that racism affords her in her everyday interactions with others. Johnson reiterates the importance of owning the power assigned to us through oppressive social systems and argues that these systems must be continually reproduced (by us) in order to survive. By extension, he asserts that oppression is frequently perpetuated not through individual acts of malice, but through the largely unconscious willingness of (otherwise well-intentioned) citizens to "go along with" established patterns of interpersonal interaction.

This book has attempted to articulate the role of the body in perpetuating these patterns, and to underscore how attention to unconscious body patterning can illuminate our approach to social justice practice and inform future research on oppression. Because the body can offer us direct access to the implicit dimensions of oppressive social interactions, it is a crucial source of knowledge in the challenging process of owning social power and privilege.

Until more targeted research is undertaken, the cycle of embodied critical learning and transformation can be employed to inquire about embodied privilege as well as embodied oppression. My work with both individuals and groups suggests that addressing issues of privilege is best undertaken after exploring experiences of oppression, rather than before. I have found that the validation and empowerment arising from articulating the wounds of injustice in a supportive environment can be a necessary strengthening precondition for the humbling experience of admitting (to oneself and others) that we benefit from the relative disadvantages of others, whether we intend to or not. Asking the client/student about hidden or unexamined resources in the embodied reflection stage of the cycle can sometimes raise the issue of privilege in a way that feels more organic to the overall exploration and less like an imposed interrogation by the facilitator.

Likewise, I often find it helpful in the embodied meaning-making phase to untangle conceptually the experiential differences between impact and intention. Recognizing that the harmful impact of enacted privilege does not require our intention to do harm can help make it easier to keep ourselves on the hook for the consequences of our behavior without succumbing to an overload of shame and self-blame. The following example illustrates one way I have worked with embodied privilege using the cycle.

A student in a graduate course I teach on embodied social justice was exploring an incident in which a conflict had arisen with a friend in deciding how to spend a weekend afternoon together. The friend had suggested a romantic comedy at the local movie theatre, but my student, who identifies as lesbian, wasn't interested in seeing a film about a heterosexual couple. My student then suggested going shopping for clothes, but the friend refused. After several tense minutes on the phone, the two friends decided not to get together after all, and their friendship has been strained ever since.

Using the cycle, my student explored the feelings that arose when her straight friend seemed not to recognize the privilege of having most popular culture references to romantic relationships represent her own sexual orientation. In particular, my student located feelings of numbness and shame in her heart and genitals, and generated a somatic experiment of imagining her strong spine connecting her heart and genitals to offer them support in the face of a culture that is still significantly homophobic. I then asked if my student wanted to explore the part of the conversation where her friend had refused to go clothes shopping. In the reflection phase, my student touched into some anger, and wondered if her friend had refused to go along simply out of spite – in a knee-jerk reaction to my student refusing to see the movie. At that point, I asked my student if there were any unexamined assets or privileges that might be informing the situation. After a long pause, my student looked up at me and said, "She's fat. My friend is really fat. She didn't want to go clothes shopping because none of the clothes will fit her and she will feel ashamed of her size." At that point, my student realized that her own size privilege had perhaps contributed to the impasse just as much as her friend's straight privilege had. As a next step, she resolved to have a conversation with her friend to explore her perceptions of the disagreement, and to broach the topic of privilege so that she could acknowledge her insensitivity in suggesting a shared activity that her friend was not likely to enjoy.

This example underscores the importance of an intersectional understanding of oppression and the attendant ability to recognize how our relative privileges and disadvantages shift according to relational context. Because my student had already grasped that her very real oppression based on sexual orientation did not exempt her from holding privilege in other social domains (she was also, for example, cisgender and able-bodied), she was able to recognize the advantages she enjoyed as someone whose body size conformed to current social norms.

To prepare clients/students to examine the issue of embodied privilege, I frequently suggest they create an inventory of social assets related to their body; that is, privilege that attaches simply to how their bodies look and function. Many will identify skin color, physical "attractiveness," athletic skill, and good health, and will then begin to unpack the subtle and arbitrary features of such privilege; for example, the size of one's feet or the shape of one's nose. Still others will recognize how these bodily "advantages" are relative to the particular social contexts in which one lives. Eli Clare (2001) provides a compelling example of such relativity in articulating how the ability to walk marks him as privileged within his community of people with cerebral palsy, even as his unsteady gait and shaking hands mark him as disabled in other contexts.

I often pair the above exercise with a body mapping exercise in which clients/ students populate an outline drawing of their body with the strengths and gifts they experience somatically, through interoception, proprioception, and reclaimed body image. They are then able to contrast the unearned assets of socially assigned body privilege with the lived experience of their body as sensitive, sensual, articulate, and intrinsically beautiful. For example, one client created a body map that featured two striking images: masses of long blond hair and a very detailed depiction of her feet. She explained that her hair was an asset that she held by virtue of its social currency – it marked her as Northern European and normatively female. In contrast, her "ugly" feet were a gift that she had intentionally cultivated, looking beyond their bumps and callouses to experience their strength and their capacity to help her feel grounded. As a professional dancer, she enjoyed both aspects of her body but was able to recognize the social privilege that attached to her hair as well as the functional beauty of her feet.

Reclaiming body image

One of the key themes emerging from the body stories presented in Part I was how profoundly experiences of oppression have shaped participants' body image. The areas of concern for the participants focused on body weight and fat oppression, skin color and racism, and physical attractiveness, appropriateness, and competence. In each case, the participants struggled to untangle externally imposed ideas about bodies from their own lived embodiment. When I teach this work, body image usually emerges as one of the most deeply painful sources of pain and confusion for students and clients.

Unfortunately, it is not uncommon to mistake social norms about bodies as also physically natural, psychologically healthy, and morally right. As a result, it can be easy to minimize the cost required to bring the body into compliance with social norms of physical appearance and comportment – it's just the appropriate (professional, respectable, decent, etc.) thing to do, right? Many of us engage in practices that impair body functions such as breathing, swallowing, and walking (for example, by wearing ties, girdles, bras, and high heels) and some create permanent alterations in body structure (through cosmetic surgery, circumcision, and ear piercing, for example). We alter our gaits, restrict our bodily expression, and discipline our shapes. These practices are frequently understood as normal and benign when they help our bodies to conform to social norms, such that similar practices employed to transgress current body norms (tattoos, scarification, chest binding, or gender reassignment surgery, for example) are often consequentially seen as excessive or even pathological. Likewise, it can be tempting to dismiss how frequently we judge the worth of others based on the degree to which they conform to prevailing body image ideals.

Of course, even with the vast array of body technologies currently available to us, not all bodily features can be modified. Those whose bodies fall irrevocably outside social norms by virtue of their skin color, anatomical structure, or physiological functioning, for example, have fewer means through which to comply with social imperatives of body image, as do those whose limited resources do not include the time and money for high-status clothes, grooming, surgery, exercise, or diet. Although we may take pleasure in the creative process of expressing ourselves (and our sociocultural identifications) through body image work, the pressure to conform to a dominant set of ideals undermines the freedom required for true creative expression for many of us.

One of the aims of an embodied approach to social justice is to introduce a stronger element of free choice into the practice of bodily expression. In so doing, this approach provides a means for disrupting social norms of the body, not by expanding the repertoire of socially acceptable body images, but by working to disable the act of body norming itself. This disabling can be facilitated by a turn toward the lived, felt experience of the body and an intentional cultivation of the body's authoritative knowledge. In so doing, we are better able to decipher and differentiate between inner bodily experience and imposed external references and imperatives about the body. By privileging sensation, attending to movement impulses, and honoring bodily intuition, we access a subjective data set that informs our relationship to objective body standards, and allows for a broader and more intentional range of possibilities.

The cycle of embodied critical learning and transformation can be used to address body image concerns and engage the process of decolonizing the body. In the following example, I highlight the embodied reflection, meaning-making, and experimentation phases in a process that harnesses our innate capacities for interoception, imagery, and creative transformation. When coupled with a critical awareness of body image norms, this process offers an opportunity to identify how these external demands colonize our subjective experience of the body.

During a weekend workshop on oppression and body image, I asked participants to reflect on how their feelings and attitudes toward their own bodies have been shaped by the social norms and expectations they encounter from their peers, family members, and communities. Through a guided interoception exercise, I helped to facilitate the gathering of an overall felt sense of the issues and concerns they held with respect to their own body image, and then asked them to allow an internal symbolic image to emerge that captured, for them, the essence of that concern. Rather than ask them to describe or draw that image, I instead asked them to bring that image in the form of an object to class the following day. The next morning, as the group members were sharing their body image objects with one another, three of them stood out.

A tall, slim young man brought a toothpick; he explained that he had been bullied as a child for being skinny, and that his schoolmates would taunt him with the nickname "Toothpick." An older Asian-American woman brought a kimono and informed the group that she was struggling with the traditional gender presentation expected of her by family members. In particular, she noted how the kimono restricted her body movements and made it hard for her to breathe. Although she did not wear a kimono in her everyday life, it symbolized for her the bodily comportment she felt she was expected to emulate. And a young Middle Eastern woman brought a shaving razor. Placing the razor in front of her, she confided to the group that she shaved her face every day to remove the visible beard and mustache that grew there. The razor symbolized for her both the hairless feminine body ideals of the North American culture into which she had immigrated, as well as her means of assimilation.

Having group members externalize and (literally) objectify an internalized body norm can make it easier for them to recognize the source of their body shame as something that came initially from outside of themselves, within social and cultural contexts that are laden with authorial power. It can also facilitate the creative exploration of that body norm in ways that allow it to transform. In most of the cases I have witnessed, that transformation does not entail an outright rejection of the body norm – for example, snapping the toothpick, shredding the kimono, or throwing away the razor. Rather, the transformation takes place in more subtle and inventive ways. In this example, I asked group members to consider ways that their body image object might transform by asking their body what it needed to feel more okay about this whole "body image" thing. (As you can see, I am drawing on one of the six *focusing* steps here to move into the engaged experimentation phase, and employing casual language to support a more relaxed and comfortable approach to serious and often painful issues.)

In the case of the young man, he reported back that his internalized toothpick image had become a sapling, with roots that grew into the ground, a trunk that supported his spine, and branches that were still small but beginning to spread. He noted with some humor that if he was going to be made of wood, at least he could be living wood. The woman with the kimono reached forward and loosened the obi (the wide panel of fabric that wraps around the waist). She stated that she was still going to wear the (symbolic) kimono, but that she also wanted to be able to breathe. And the young woman with the razor decided to pass it around the circle, allowing each group member to hold it in turn. She hasn't yet made up her mind whether she is going to continue to remove her facial hair, but remarked that the most painful aspect of this issue for her was the secrecy that surrounded it. Now when she holds the razor while shaving, she can imagine the imprint of those other hands, and remember the support and understanding she felt from the group.

In each case, participants identified a source of pain connected to an internalized body norm (that is, a belief about the body that originates from outside the self but is taken into the self, even when it causes pain). In choosing an external object to symbolize the body norm, they reexternalized it, making it available for reflection and critique by themselves and others.

Although this example is one way to work with reclaiming body image, I have also used the cycle of embodied critical learning and transformation to help clients and students unpack experiences where body image was not an intentional focus (as it was in this example) but instead an important but previously unrecognized feature of a larger event. In those cases, remembering to inquire about body image during the embodied reflection phase can help bring these issues to the surface.

Somatic resourcing, resistance, and resilience

> Caring for myself is not self-indulgence, it is self-preservation, and that is an act of political warfare.
>
> *(Lorde, 1988, p. 131)*

As noted in the introduction to this chapter, if embodied social justice work is to be truly transformative, the models and processes we employ should not only serve to repair the damage done to individuals but must also generate strategies for resistance that affect the collective. In this section, I outline a sequence that embeds these strategies within a process that includes resourcing and resilience as crucial elements of a sustainable strategy for social change.

Resourcing

Resourcing is a concept that figures prominently in the Somatic Experiencing® (SE) work developed by trauma expert Peter Levine (2010). In SE, clients are encouraged to connect with sources of pleasure, comfort, stability, and reassurance before tackling the challenging work of exploring and resolving the impact of past traumatic events. Resourcing recognizes that unpacking trauma is potentially destabilizing, and that being able to return to a bodily sense of safety in the present moment can help to prevent the exploration of past traumas from overwhelming the client and potentially reinforcing (rather than undoing) the trauma response.

Although the cycle of embodied critical learning and transformation is different from the process of trauma resolution employed in SE, the two models share a focus on interoception and proprioception as core elements (Payne et al., 2015). I have already noted in previous chapters the research literature (including my own work) that supports the idea of oppression as traumatic, and have found the notion of resourcing extremely helpful in working through the embodied impact of oppression.

When I facilitate the use of the cycle with individuals and groups, I nearly always begin with a formal acknowledgement of the value of resourcing in social justice work and then introduce exercises to help everyone (including myself) connect with our bodily capacities for feeling centered, grounded, balanced, and awake. I repeat this resourcing process as needed, particularly before and after the engaging/experimenting phase. New ways of being in our body and in the world are rarely enacted without some risk, and resourcing beforehand can help mitigate the impact of that risk and make innovative behaviors easier to attempt.

Another reason I emphasize resourcing before risk is that the act of connecting with our bodily sense of strength, safety, and comfort is also an excellent way to rekindle our capacities for embodied sensitivity, presence, integrity, and attunement. Through resourcing – where we connect with pleasure[2] and a sense of stability – we come home to our bodies. We remember ourselves and reconnect with a bodily sense of knowing and integrity. Grounded in the delicate fierceness of our tissues, we are better able to hold space for the vulnerabilities and drives of other bodies. In other words, a necessary precondition for resistance is to occupy ourselves.

Resistance

In an earlier section, I discussed strategies for reclaiming body image and how the cycle of embodied learning and transformation could be used in the service of decolonizing the body. Through this process of embodied reclaiming and decolonization, we begin, literally, to reshape ourselves. Although often generated on an interoceptive level, changes to our internal body image initiate changes in our postural and movement repertoire. Perhaps the shoulders that were hunched begin to release and rest gently on the ribcage. Perhaps the ribcage that was held immobile begins to expand and release, or the breath that was shallow deepens. The pelvis swings, the feet dig in, the knees spread, and the gaze intensifies. Although these bodily shifts could be understood simply as a process of individual change, their impact always occurs on a relational level as well. Merleau-Ponty's notion of intercorporeality and more recent neuroscientific research remind us that we are hard-wired to be affected by the embodied expressions of others. In other words, changes in embodiment that transgress social norms are inherently acts of resistance.

The nonverbal communication literature describes posture, gesture, and other bodily behaviors in terms of their relationship to dominant or subordinate social status (Ellyson and Dovidio, 1985). Examples of dominant nonverbal communication in Western societies include direct eye contact, direct and pointed gestures, and expansive posture, while subordinate behaviors include indirect gaze and gestures and constricted posture. In developing strategies for embodied acts of resistance, therefore, it might be tempting for members of subordinated social groups to resist their oppression by adopting the nonverbal communication styles of the dominant social group. Take up a longer stride, commandeer more space on the subway, and never be the first person to blink. Although there is nothing inherently problematic in these actions, unless the impulse to move in such a way emerges from a bodily felt sense of rightness and integrity, they will likely function more as empty gestures than as authentic expressions.

I'm not suggesting here that there is no value in the "fake it until you make it" school of behavioral change; it sometimes requires many attempts to feel truly comfortable in enacting forms of embodiment that are new or challenging. *I am, however, advocating an organic process of developing strategies for embodied resistance that are anchored in a deeply felt sense of one's own body embedded in the particular sociocultural context of one's own life.* In this way, it seems more likely that the enacted behaviors will serve as insubordinating patterns, rather than simply as a substitution of subordinating patterns for dominating patterns.

For example, at a panel presentation at a recent conference on body psychotherapy, I offered one of my own strategies for embodied resistance to the audience. To illustrate it, I moved from behind the long table where the panelists were seated and sat in a chair off to the side of the stage with my legs spread wide and my feet firmly anchored to the floor. In this single move, I simultaneously disrupted conventional spatial power arrangements (where speakers were located front and center as a sign of their authority) and transgressed gender norms by adopting a posture that would likely be read by the audience as insufficiently feminine. Within seconds and without words, nearly everyone immediately seemed to grasp the social implications of what I had done; gasps, nods, chuckles, and sighs bubbled up throughout the room as audience members at the back stood up and craned their necks to see what the fuss was about. From my perspective, this immediate grasp was possible, in part, because I was completely present and comfortable in my body when I did it, and thus could clearly observe the space between my own agency and the persistent expectation made evident by the audience's response. To be clear, it's not that I learned how to be comfortable sitting with my legs apart even though I had been socialized as a young girl to sit with my knees together. It's that when I am feeling completely comfortable in my own skin, that is how I sit.

When facilitating the engaging/experimenting phase of the cycle of embodied critical learning and transformation (which is the place where most strategies for embodied resistance tend to emerge), I pay particular attention to supporting the individual client/student to feel into the new behavioral patterns as they enact them. I try to help them recognize that insubordinating body postures and movements might feel strange and scary at first, but they should also still feel – somewhere deep inside – *right*. Drawing upon and trusting the authoritative knowledge of their own body will help them create an expression of resistance to oppression that is uniquely and fittingly theirs. Of course, there can be serious repercussions for occupying one's own skin, including violence, discrimination, and harassment. I am not arguing here that being fully and consciously embodied overturns oppression, but that being in one's skin is a powerful tool for empowerment against oppression, such that we can experience our body as our fierce ally as opposed to that which shames and betrays us.

Resilience

Although the notion of embodied resilience has its complications (as I noted in the introduction to this chapter), it is the term I have come to use when describing the iterative effects of multiple cycles of resourcing and resistance. Through a process of inquiry and discovery linked to action, we learn how to access the potency and integrity of our own embodied experience. With the discerning support of others, we find the courage to refuse the social constraints imposed on our bodies and mend some of the personal damage that oppression inflicts. To the extent that we can, we learn to protect our internal experience of self from further harm and work to prevent injury to others. Over time, resilience comes to be embodied as the capacity to hold fast to our hearts in the midst of trouble and the ability to return to center and ground when the world tries to pull us away from our core values; from what we know in our bones.

In my experience, however, resilience does not accrue only through the repeated practice of resourcing and resistance – it can be proactively cultivated. In observing the ways in which some clients/students embody resilience despite extensive exposure to oppressive social systems and limited access to supportive resources, I have come to identify some body-based capacities that seem to help these individuals develop the ability to navigate extremely challenging circumstances with stamina, patience, and even some grace. These capacities include:

1. The ability to "witness" (that is, to sense and feel with an attitude of open curiosity and compassion) one's own embodied experience in stillness, while in motion, and in various relational and environmental contexts.[3]
2. Correspondingly, the ability to "witness" the embodied experience of others and to be "witnessed" by them. In other words, the capacity to co-create and maintain an attuned body-to-body relational frame in which you are simultaneously present to yourself and others.
3. The ability to get "grounded" and "centered" in the body; in other words, to engage in a process of somatic self-regulation when in a state of sympathetic nervous system overwhelm.[4]
4. The ability to take pleasure in embodied experience and appreciate its aesthetic qualities.
5. The ability to engage in ethical decision-making informed by embodied empathy and integrity; that is, the capacity to engage one's embodied core values in considering the needs and demands of others.[5]
6. The ability to learn from (identify, reflect upon, make meaning of, transform, and integrate) individual, relational, and collective experiences in and through the body by working the cycle of embodied critical learning and transformation.

It is important to understand the development of these capacities as unique to each individual in the context of their relational and sociocultural contexts, and to recognize the dangers of assuming universal norms of embodiment or Western standards of "competence," "ethics," or "aesthetics," for example. These capacities should also be contextualized to recognize the neurological and anatomical diversity that is a normal expression of human biology and to incorporate sociocultural differences and an analysis of how power differentials affect embodiment. In other words, while these capacities may serve as useful guides for individuals wishing to strengthen their resilience in the face of adversity and discrimination, there are no universal standards by which these capacities should be measured. In cultivating them, each person decides for themselves how and when these abilities might be realized. For those wishing to pursue this in more detail, Chapter 13 offers information about established embodiment practices that are designed to develop and nurture one or more of these capacities.

To conclude this section, I offer a final, small body story taken from a post on a blog I co-host with my colleague Diane Israel, entitled *Queer Habitus*.[6] In this narrative, I articulate one way that resourcing, resistance, and resilience come together in the creation and navigation of personal space.

An integrative example: cultivating the intimate kinesphere

One of the ways I "queer" how culture intersects with my bodily experience is that I don't understand sensual experience in quite the same way that many people do – that is, as an extension of (or precursor to) sexual interaction. For me, sensual experience tends to center on my relationship with my own body, rather than on my relationship with another person's body.

For the most part, my experience of sensual pleasure occurs within an area around my body that I call my "intimate kinesphere." A kinesphere is a movement term coined by choreographer and movement analyst Rudolph Laban that refers to the roughly spherical space around a body that extends as far as that body can reach without traveling through space. I use the term "intimate kinesphere" to define a smaller area that refers to a bubble of space around my body radiating like an aura about a foot from the surface of my skin. Within this space, it is possible to hear me breathe, feel my body warmth, smell me, and almost touch me – which is why I call it "intimate."

I rarely allow people into my intimate kinesphere unless I trust them, and will often exclude others from this space even when I know them well. Like many who experience marginalization from mainstream society, I can be pretty vigilant about monitoring the nonverbal behavior of other human beings in my proximal social space. I nearly always track the spatial relationships between myself and others, and can be exquisitely sensitive to signals of dominance and aggression. For example, I will often position myself in a room where I can observe the subtleties of gesture that identify those members of the group who are accorded deference by virtue of their social privilege, in order to avoid interacting with them. Although I am committed to being respectful of others, I am disinclined toward deference, even as a defensive posture, and vastly prefer to be excluded than to be accepted at the cost of submission.

Although it's guarded by vigilant awareness and instinctive withdrawal should the boundaries be breached, my intimate kinesphere is also where I spend a lot of time hanging out. To put it another way, I "cultivate the space." Many of my gestures occur in this space, and I pay particular attention to the sights, sounds, textures, and smells that happen inside it. When I breathe, I imagine the air circulating inside that space.

The more I cultivate my intimate kinesphere, the deeper and more complex a territory it becomes. The clothes I wear form an important part of my kinesphere, providing me with a rich and nuanced source of color, texture, and movement. When I wear scent, it is intended to infuse the space around me but not extend beyond that space or intrude into the spaces of others. Within this small space, I indulge in the textures of my hair and skin, enjoy the movement of my limbs, and connect to myself through touch. I peel an orange and inhale the tangy mist of the rind and lick the juice from my fingers. I hum quietly to myself.

The cultivation of this personal space is for my own sensual pleasure. It provides me with nourishment in an industrialized, urban social setting that often feels impoverished and impoverishing. So, for the most part, my sensual pleasure has nothing to do with anyone else. Put another way, I'm not stroking my neck and breathing deeply on your account. If I'm doing these things in your presence at all, it's because I'm comfortable enough with you to let you witness the sensuality of my relationship with my body.

What does this mean for those of us who are exploring a somatic stance as a form of social activism? For me, reclaiming the felt experience of my body is a political act in a postmodern world that commodifies bodies as tools and assets or reads them as symbolic texts. In cultivating my intimate kinesphere, I claim some space in a social world that often pushes me to the margins. And by insisting on my right to take sustenance in my own pleasure, I queer what I have been taught about what sensuality should be.

Unlike most of the previous examples in this chapter, this passage does not explicitly identify the various concepts it is intended to illustrate. Rather, this articulation of the embodied experience points to how aspects of resourcing, resistance, and resilience can be interwoven and embedded within other topics (in this case, conscious embodiment and the use of personal space). This passage also suggests the qualities of vulnerability and sensitivity that undergird a position of strength. This strength should not be understood as a defense against weakness, but as a commitment to self-actualization that includes our tenderness and our irrevocable woundedness. By framing resilience as such a commitment – as a radical act that keeps us fully present in a world that both refuses and requires our presence – it is possible to shift "self-care" from feeling like an additional weight on the already overburdened to becoming the non-negotiable bedrock of our activism.

As with the other features of living in oppressive social systems discussed in this book, the role of the body in cultivating resilience should be understood as an often-overlooked resource, rather than the only source of sustenance. The lived felt experience of our bodies can be a wellspring of sensory nourishment, but so too can art, nature, and the company of loved ones. Finding ways to harness our bodily capacity for renewal and realignment simply enhances the strategies we have available to support our ongoing resilience and the resilience of those clients and students with whom we work.

Gathering up and moving forward

Embodied Social Justice describes the embodied experiences of individuals who have faced various forms of oppression, and connects those experiences to implications for social justice in an increasingly complex and challenging world. Although the body stories in this book offer examples of the trauma, shame, and disconnection that result from the abuse and misuse of social power, they also offer the promise of personal and collective change. Despite the embodied wounds inflicted through unjust and inequitable power relations, the participants in my research (as well as my clients and students over the years) still experience their bodies as important sources of knowledge and power. By reconnecting to the breathing, beating hearts of ourselves and aligning with the sensitivity and vulnerability of our flesh, we can embody a different kind of strength.

This book also emphasizes how oppression is learned and unlearned through the body. The findings of my research suggest that learning theories and practices can provide a useful framework for addressing and transforming social oppression, and that learning which includes the body has important implications for social justice praxis. These implications, articulated through the development of a model of embodied critical learning and transformation, emphasize the importance of regaining access to the felt experience of the body and underscore the possibilities for social change that emerge from the project of intentional embodiment as a form of critical consciousness. The model of embodied critical learning and transformation described in this book offers one way to work with the embodied experience of oppression that focuses on the lived experience of the oppressed, and offers strategies for grasping and transforming that experience. By working together in a process of inquiry (rather than certainty) and collaboration (rather than isolation) it might become possible to step away from the entrenched positions and polarized relational patterns that reproduce oppression and result in so much pain, fear, and mistrust. Harnessing the intelligence of our bodies in this task will allow us to make these shifts authentically and concretely, so that we are never in the same place after our explorations as we were when we began.

Social justice remains one of our most pressing and intransigent issues, especially in the face of escalating threats to the global environment and international human rights. Although continued efforts to dismantle oppression on a systemic level must continue, these efforts are supported by also working at the everyday, micro-sociological level. With the increasing recognition of the body's role in social interactions, a more embodied approach to anti-oppression work is a timely addition to the tools and strategies already in use among helping professionals. This book offers preliminary ideas about how the project of unlearning the lived experience of oppression might proceed, and I hope that it will serve as a useful and encouraging point of reference for counselors, educators, community activists, and others who are interested in engaging the body's capacity to transform the world.

Notes

1 See, for example, Balme et al. (2015).
2 For those who experience chronic physical pain or limitation, resourcing through the body can sometimes be challenging. In my own experience dealing with chronic pain

and mobility limitations (see Chapter 7), as with some of the narratives emerging from critical disability studies, cultivating strength and pleasure in a relatively unaffected body area seems to be one way to engage the body as a resource. For example, even when I was experiencing constant pain in my knees, I could still consciously enjoy the feeling of nimbleness and sensitivity in my hands.

3 The somatic practices of Authentic Movement and Sensory Awareness work to cultivate the witness function.

4 Somatic self-regulation when in a state of sympathetic nervous system overwhelm refers to bodily practices (such as slow, deep breathing and conscious muscular relaxation) that help to calm the fight, flight, or freeze impulses that arise under conditions of threat (Ogden et al., 2006).

5 Lenore Hervey's work on embodied ethical decision-making is a helpful resource here (e.g. Hervey, 2007).

6 Available at: https://queerhabitus.wordpress.com/.

13

COMMUNITY RESOURCES

As noted in previous chapters, the implications for practice that emerge from an embodied approach to social justice extend well beyond the development of models and the application of techniques. As practitioners and community members, we must commit to the cultivation of our own capacities as engaged and embodied beings who recognize the impact of oppression on our own bodies and undertake to heal the personal and relational damage and prevent further harm. Doing our own work allows us to work with others with integrity (that is, by walking the walk) and offers us some protection from burnout by reconnecting with our bodies as sources of knowledge and power. Fortunately, many somatic approaches to professional development (academic degree programs, training programs, conferences, and workshops) employ a pedagogical approach that experientially anchors the material being taught in the bodies of participants, so that professional development is always simultaneously personal development and vice versa. In this chapter, I offer links to some current resources that human service professionals might find helpful in developing their knowledge and skills in embodied approaches to social justice.

Specialized training resources

The professional trainings listed below represent approaches that have already integrated the body with trauma, conflict, or social justice.

Programs in embodiment and social justice

- Embodied Liberation (www.embodiedliberation.com) Dedicated to offering ideas, writing, workshops, and unequivocal encouragement as we navigate the intensity of the tensions between terror and safety, oppression and justice, love and liberation.

- Embodied Social Justice (www.embodiedsocialjustice.com) Provides training and consultation to organizations, agencies, and schools on the approach to embodied social justice outlined in this book, using the cycle of embodied critical learning and transformation.
- Embody Deep Democracy (www.embodydeepdemocracy.com) Aims to bring deeper awareness and engagement to feeling, imagination, ancestors, spiritual knowing; an intelligence that precedes experiences of colonization, apartheid, or oppression.
- Generative Somatics (www.generativesomatics.org) Offers training in a form of politicized somatics that draws on embodied practices to create social change by linking individual experiences of trauma to the social contexts in which we live.
- Interplay (www.interplay.org) Offers workshop intensives on embodiment and racism called *Changing the Race Dance*, which aim to offer participants and opportunity to "engage in empowering opportunities to address race and racism and unpack inequity with fewer words and more wisdom."
- Moving on Center (www.movingoncenter.org) A training program linking somatics and the performing arts for social change. Using experiential and cooperative learning, Moving on Center has a mission to develop community leaders and artists who engage the whole body–mind to promote holistic social change.

Embodied leadership and peacemaking

- Center for Movement Education and Research (www.cmer.info) Embodied Leadership Training (ELT) incorporates the best practices from somatics, movement studies, and mindfulness while also providing models for personal development work using issues clearing, non-violent communication, and voice dialogue.
- Embody Peace (www.embodypeace.wordpress.com) Connecting organizations and individuals who engage in peace-making through the embodied arts, movement, and body awareness.
- Leadership Embodiment (www.embodimentinternational.com) A coaching program that uses principles from the non-violent Japanese martial art of aikido and mindfulness to offer simple tools and practices to increase leadership presence and respond to stress and pressure with greater confidence and integrity.
- Strozzi Institute (www.strozziinstitute.com) Offers training in somatic coaching and embodied leadership to produce leaders and organizations who can use conflict as a generative force.

Somatic approaches to trauma

- Neuro-Affective Relational Model (www.body-mindtherapy.com/narm/) An advanced clinical training for mental health and somatic practitioners who work with developmental trauma.

- Sensorimotor Psychotherapy (www.sensorimotorpsychotherapy.org) A professional educational organization that designs and provides trainings and services to serve a global network of mental health practitioners.
- Somatic Experiencing Trauma Institute (www.traumahealing.org) A nonprofit organization dedicated to resolving trauma worldwide by providing professional training and public education in Somatic Experiencing®.

Professional organizations with approved somatic training programs

For readers who already have a background in social justice work but would like to enhance their skills by gaining certification in a somatic education or therapy modality, several organizations certify training programs around the world.

- International Somatic Movement Education and Therapy Association (ISMETA; www.ismeta.org/ismeta-approved-training-programs/) Over twenty-five professional training programs in North America and Europe meet ISMETA requirements for registration as a somatic movement therapist or somatic movement educator.
- United States Association of Body Psychotherapy (USABP; www.usabp.org/education-training/) Over twenty academic and professional training programs are members of the USABP.
- European Association of Body Psychotherapy (EABP; www.eabp.org/forum.php) Over twenty training institutes are currently accredited through the EABP.
- American Dance Therapy Association (ADTA; www.adta.org) The ADTA approves Master's programs in dance therapy and offers an alternate route toward registration as a dance movement therapist.

Academic programs

A small number of academic institutions offer graduate degree programs in somatic counseling psychology, dance movement therapy, and somatic studies, including the California Institute of Integral Studies, Naropa University, Pacifica Graduate Institute, the University of Lancashire, Lesley University, Drexel University, and Antioch University, New England. Although the clinical counseling/psychology programs at these universities offer coursework in multicultural and diversity issues, none currently offer a specific social justice focus. Conversely, the numerous graduate programs in social work, education, and community mental health that specialize in social justice do not currently focus on the body. That said, a handful of academics working on the topic of embodied social justice across a range of disciplines mentor students in this area. The following sections may help practitioners identify those authors with whom they might wish to pursue further study.

Academic and professional journals

Several journals focus on a somatic or embodied perspective:

- *Body and Society*
- *Body, Movement, and Dance in Psychotherapy*
- *International Journal of Body Psychotherapy*
- *Journal of Dance and Somatic Practices*
- *Somatics Journal*

A number of academic and professional publications focus on social justice:

- *International Journal of Critical Pedagogy*
- *Journal of Critical and Radical Social Work*
- *Journal of Critical Psychology, Counselling and Psychotherapy*
- *Studies in Social Justice*

Conferences

Professional and academic conferences are beginning to focus on the body and social justice. Some recent events include:

- Embodying Social Justice: Contemporary Perspectives across the Arts and Psychological Therapies, co-sponsored by the University of Roehampton
- Dance and Social Justice Conference, sponsored by Gallatin School of Individualized Study at New York University
- Yoga and Social Justice Conference, sponsored by the Yoga and Body Image Coalition

Recommended reading

In addition to the titles listed in the Bibliography, there are several texts that I frequently recommend or assign to my graduate students:

Abram, D. (1996). *The spell of the sensuous.* New York: Vintage Books.

Barratt, B. B. (2013). *The emergence of somatic psychology and bodymind therapy: Critical theory and practice in psychology and the human sciences.* London: Palgrave Macmillan.

Eddy, M. (2016). *Mindful movement: The evolution of the somatic arts and conscious action.* Chicago: University of Chicago Press.

Johnson, D. (1997). *Groundworks: Narratives of embodiment.* Berkeley, CA: North Atlantic Books.

Olsen, A. (1991). *Bodystories: A guide to experiential anatomy.* Barrytown, NY: Station Hill Press.

Tangenberg, K. M., and Kemp, S. (2002). Embodied practice: Claiming the body's experience, agency, and knowledge for social work. *Social Work*, 47(1), 9–18.

BIBLIOGRAPHY

Ali, Mahershala. (2017). Screen Actors' Guild award acceptance speech. Retrieved from www.gq.com/story/mahershala-ali-sag-acceptance-speech, accessed March 30, 2017.

Ali-Khan, C. (2016). Dirty secrets and silent conversations: Exploring radical listening through embodied autoethnographic teaching. *International Journal of Critical Pedagogy*, 7(3). Retrieved from http://libjournal.uncg.edu/ijcp/article/view/1319/1012, accessed March 29, 2017.

American Psychiatric Association. (1994). *DSM-IV-TR: Diagnostic and statistical manual of mental disorders*. Washington, DC: American Psychiatric Association.

American Psychiatric Association. (2013). *DSM V: Diagnostic and statistical manual of mental disorders*. Washington, DC: American Psychiatric Association.

Anderson, R. (2002a). Embodied writing: Presencing the body in somatic research, Part I, What is embodied writing. *Somatics Magazine–Journal of the Mind/Body Arts and Sciences*, 13(4), 40–44.

Anderson, R. (2002b). Embodied writing: Presencing the body in somatic research, Part II, Research Applications. *Somatics Magazine–Journal of the Mind/Body Arts and Sciences*, 14(1), 40–44.

Argyle, M. (2013). *Bodily communication*. New York: Routledge.

Atkins, D. (Ed.). (1998). *Looking queer: Body image and identity in lesbian, bisexual, gay, and transgender communities*. Binghamton, NY: Haworth Press.

Balme, E., Gerada, C., and Page, L. (2015). Doctors need to be supported, not trained in resilience. *BMJ Careers*, September 15. Retrieved from http://careers.bmj.com/careers/a dvice/Doctors_need_to_be_supported,_not_trained_in_resilience, accessed March 30, 2017.

Bartky, S. L. (1989). *Shame and gender: Contribution to a phenomenology of oppression*. Milwaukee: University of Wisconsin-Milwaukee Center for Twentieth Century Studies.

Beaudoin, C. (1999). Integrating somatic learning into everyday life. *Canadian Journal of Education*, 24(1), 76–80.

Beckett, D., and Morris, G. (2001). Ontological performance: Bodies, identities and learning. *Studies in the Education of Adults*, 33(1), 35–48.

Behnke, E. A. (1995). Matching. In D. H. Johnson (Ed.), *Bone, breath, and gesture: Practices of embodiment*, pp. 317–337. Berkeley, CA: North Atlantic Books.

Berila, B. (2015). *Integrating mindfulness into anti-oppression pedagogy: Social justice in higher education*. New York: Routledge.

Birdwhistell, R. L. (1970). *Kinesics and context: Essays on body motion communication*. Philadelphia: University of Pennsylvania Press.

Blume, E. S. (1990). *Secret survivors*. New York: Wiley.

Bordo, S. (1993). *Unbearable weight*. Berkeley: University of California Press.

Boud, D. (1985). *Reflection: Turning experience into learning*. London: Kogan Page.

Bourdieu, P. (1980). Structures, *habitus*, practices. In *The Logic of Practice* (translated by Richard Nice), pp. 52–65. Stanford, CT: Stanford University Press.

Brockman, J. (2001). A somatic epistemology for education. *Educational Forum*, 65(4), 328–334.

Bryant-Davis, T., and Ocampo, C. (2005). Racist incident-based trauma. *The Counseling Psychologist*, 33(4), 479–500.

Burgoon, J. K., Guerrero, L. K., and Floyd, K. (2016). *Nonverbal communication*. New York: Routledge.

Burstow, B. (1992). *Radical feminist therapy: Working in the context of violence*. Thousand Oaks, CA: Sage.

Burstow, B. (2002). Creative empowerment with the disenfranchised. In the personal collection of Bonnie Burstow, Ontario Institute for Studies in Education, University of Toronto.

Burstow, B. (2003). Toward a radical understanding of trauma and trauma work. *Violence Against Women*, 9(11), 1293–1317.

Butler, J. (1990). *Gender trouble: Feminism and the subversion of identity*. New York: Routledge.

Butler, J. (1993). *Bodies that matter: On the discursive limits of sex*. New York: Routledge.

Caldwell, C. (In press). Micro-movements. In H. Payne, J. Tantia, and S. Koch (Eds.), *Embodied perspectives in psychotherapy*. London: Routledge.

Campbell, J., and Moyers, B. (2011). *The power of myth*. New York: Doubleday.

Chadwick, R. J. (2012). Fleshy enough? Notes towards an embodied analysis in critical qualitative research. *Gay and Lesbian Issues and Psychology Review*, 8(2), 82–97.

Clare, E. (2001). Stolen bodies, reclaimed bodies: Disability and queerness. *Public Culture*, 13(3): 359–365.

Cohen, B. B. (2012). *Sensing, feeling, and action: The experiential anatomy of body–mind centering*. Northampton, MA: Contact Quarterly Editions.

Cohen, J. J., and Weiss, G. (Eds.). (2003). *Thinking the limits of the body*. Albany: State University of New York Press.

Connell, R. W. (1993). *Schools and social justice*. Philadelphia: Temple University Press.

Corrigan, P. (1992). Towards new socio-semiotic directions in clothing. In M. Balat and J. Deledalle-Rhodes (Eds.), *Signs of humanity* (Vol. 2), pp. 1127–1131. Berlin and New York: Mouton de Gruyter.

Craig, A. D. (2002). How do you feel? Interoception: the sense of the physiological condition of the body. *Nature Reviews Neuroscience*, 3(8), 655–666.

Crenshaw, K. (1991). Mapping the margins: Intersectionality, identity politics, and violence against women of color. *Stanford Law Review*, 43(6), 1241–1299.

Cromwell, J. (1999). *Transmen and FTMs: Identities, bodies, genders and sexualities*. Champaign: University of Illinois Press.

Csikszentmihalyi, M. (1997). *Finding flow: The psychology of engagement with everyday life*. New York: Basic Books.

Csordas, T. (Ed.). (1994). *Embodiment and experience: The existential ground of culture and self.* Cambridge: Cambridge University Press.

Damasio, A. R. (1999). *The feeling of what happens: Body and emotion in the making of consciousness.* New York: Houghton Mifflin Harcourt.

Delgado, R., and Stefancic, J. (1997). *Critical white studies: Looking behind the mirror.* Philadelphia: Temple University Press.

Dewey, J. (1897). My pedagogic creed. *School Journal*, 3, 77–80.

Dewey, J. (1916). *Democracy and education: An introduction to philosophy of education.* New York: Macmillan.

Dewey, J. (1933). *How we think: A restatement of the relation of reflective thinking to the educational process.* Lexington, MA: Heath.

Dixon, M., and Senior, K. (2011). Appearing pedagogy: From embodied learning and teaching to embodied pedagogy. *Pedagogy, Culture and Society*, 19(3), 473–484.

Doyle, L. (2003). Ontological crisis and double narration in African American fiction: Reconstructing *Our Nig.* In J. J. Cohen and G. Weiss (Eds.), *Thinking the limits of the body*, pp. 85–100. Albany: State University of New York Press.

Drew, L. (2014). Embodied learning processes in activism *Canadian Journal for the Study of Adult Education*, 27(1), 83.

Durrance, B. (1998). Some explicit thoughts on tacit learning. *Training and Development*, 52(12), 24–30.

Ekman, P., and Friesen, W. (1969). The repertoire of nonverbal behavior: Categories, origins, usage and codings. *Semiotics*, 1, 49–98.

Eliot, P., and Roen, K. (1998). Transgenderism and the question of embodiment: Promising queer politics? *GLQ: A Journal of Gay and Lesbian Studies*, 4(2), 231–261.

Ellyson, S. L., and Dovidio, J. (1985). *Power, dominance and nonverbal behavior.* New York: Springer-Verlag.

Ericsson, K. A., and Simon, H. A. (1998). How to study thinking in everyday life: Contrasting think-aloud protocols with descriptions and explanations of thinking. *Mind, Culture, and Activity*, 5(3), 178–186.

Farb, N., Daubenmier, J., Price, C. J., Gard, T., Kerr, C., Dunn, B. D., *et al.* (2015). Interoception, contemplative practice, and health. *Frontiers in Psychology*, 6, 763.

Finlay, L. (2005). Reflexive embodied empathy: A phenomenology of participant–researcher intersubjectivity. *The Humanistic Psychologist*, 33(4), 271–292.

Forgasz, R. (2015). Embodiment: A multimodal international teacher education pedagogy. In C. J. Craig and L. Orland-Barak (Eds.), *International teacher education: Promising pedagogies* (Vol. 22C), pp. 115–137. Bingley: Emerald Group Publishing.

Fortin, S. (1998). Somatics: A tool for empowering modern dance teachers. In S. B. Shapiro (Ed.), *Dance, power and difference: Critical and feminist perspectives on dance education*, pp. 49–74. Champaign, IL: Human Kinetics.

Foucault, M. (1990). *The history of sexuality* (Vol. 1). New York: Vintage Books.

Foucault, M. (1991). *Discipline and punish: The birth of the prison.* New York: Vintage Books.

Frank, A. (1996). *The wounded storyteller: Body, ethics, and illness.* Chicago: University of Chicago Press.

Freire, P. (2000). *Pedagogy of the oppressed* (30th anniversary edition). New York: Continuum.

Fromkin, V., and Rodman, J. (1983). *An introduction to language.* New York: CBS College Publishing.

Gallese, V. (2014). Bodily selves in relation: embodied simulation as second-person perspective on intersubjectivity. *Philosophical Transaction of the Royal Society B*, 369(1644).

Retrieved   from   http://rstb.royalsocietypublishing.org/content/369/1644/20130177, accessed March 29, 2017.

Gendlin, E. T. (1982). *Focusing*. New York: Random House.

Gendlin, E. T. (2005). *Relationality in focusing*. Video. Retrieved from https://youtu.be/Wbf97DVraUI, accessed March 30, 2017.

Gendlin, E. T. (2012). *Focusing-oriented psychotherapy: A manual of the experiential method*. London: Guilford Press.

Gershon, M. D. (1999). The enteric nervous system: A second brain. *Hospital Practice*, 34(7), 31–52.

Giddens, A. (1990). Structuration theory and sociological analysis. In J. Clark, C. Modgil, and S. Modgil (Eds.), *Anthony Giddens: Consensus and controversy*, pp. 297–315. Bristol: The Falmer Press.

Gladwell, M. (2007). *Blink: The power of thinking without thinking*. New York: Little, Brown and Company.

Godagama, S. (1997). *The handbook of Ayurveda*. London: Kyle Cathie.

Goffman, E. (1959). *The presentation of self in everyday life*. Garden City, NY: Doubleday.

Granger, D. A. (2010). Somaesthetics and racism: Toward an embodied pedagogy of difference. *Journal of Aesthetic Education*, 44(3), 69–81.

Greene, D. (1997). Assumptions of somatics, Part II. *Somatics Magazine–Journal of the Mind/Body Arts and Sciences*, 11(3), 50–54.

Grosz, E. A. (1994). *Volatile bodies: Toward a corporeal feminism*. Bloomington: Indiana University Press.

Hall, E. T. (1963). Proxemics: The study of man's spatial relations. In I. Galdston (Ed.), *Man's image in medicine and anthropology: Arden House conference on medicine and anthropology*. New York: International Universities Press.

Hall, E. T. (1974). *Handbook for proxemic research*. Washington, DC: Society for the Anthropology of Visual Communication.

Hall, J. A., and Halberstadt, A. (1986). Smiling and gazing. In J. S. Hyde and M. C. Linn (Eds.), *The psychology of gender: Advances through meta-analysis*, pp. 122–130. Baltimore: Johns Hopkins University Press.

Hanna, T. (1970). *Bodies in revolt: A primer in somatic thinking*. Novato, CA: Freeperson Press.

Hanna, T. (1988). *Somatics: Reawakening the mind's control of movement, flexibility, and health*. Reading, MA: Addison-Wesley.

Haselager, W. F. G., Broens, M. C., and Gonzalez, M. E. Q. (2012). The importance of sensing one's movement in the world for the sense of personal identity. *Rivista internazionale di Filosofia e Psicologia*, 3(1), 1–11.

Heaney, T. (1995). Issues in Freireian pedagogy. *Thresholds in Education*. www.paulofreire.ufpb.br/paulofreire/Files/outros/Issues_in_Freirean_Pedagogy.pdf, accessed March 29, 2017.

Hein, S. F. (2004). Embodied reflexivity: The disclosive capacity of the lived body. In Serge P. Sholov (Ed.), *Advances in Psychology Research*, 30, pp. 57–74. Hauppauge, NY: Nova.

Henley, N. (1977). *Body politics: Power, sex, and nonverbal communication*. Englewood Cliffs, NJ: Prentice-Hall.

Henley, N., and Freeman, J. (1995). The sexual politics of interpersonal behavior. In J. Freeman (Ed.), *Women: A feminist perspective*, pp. 89–95. London: Mayfield.

Henley, N., and LaFrance, M. (1984). Gender as culture: Difference and dominance in nonverbal behavior. In A. Wolfgang (Ed.), *Nonverbal behavior: Perspectives, applications, intercultural insights*, pp. 351–371. Lewiston, NY: C. J. Hogrefe.

Hervey, L. W. (2007). Embodied ethical decision making. *American Journal of Dance Therapy*, 29(2), 91–108.

Hickson, M., Stacks, D., and Moore, N. (2003). *Nonverbal communication studies and applications, fourth edition*. London: Roxbury.

Holst, J. (2013). Re-educating the body. *Educational Philosophy and Theory*, 45(9), 963–972.

hooks, b. (1981). *Ain't I a woman? Black women and feminism*. New York: Routledge.

hooks, b. (1994). *Teaching to transgress*. New York: Routledge.

Hopwood, N. (2017). Practice, the body and pedagogy: Attuning as a basis for pedagogies of the unknown. In P. Grootenboer, C. Edwards-Groves, and S. Choy (Eds.), *Practice theory perspectives on pedagogy and education*, pp. 87–106. Singapore: Springer.

Johnson, A. (2001). *Privilege, power, and difference*. Mountain View, CA: Mayfield Publishing.

Johnson, D. H. (1983). *Body*. Boston, MA: Beacon Press.

Johnson, D. H. (1995). *Bone, breath & gesture: Practices of embodiment* (Vol. 1). Berkeley, CA: North Atlantic Books.

Johnson, R. (2009). Oppression embodied: Exploring the intersections of somatic psychology, trauma, and oppression. *International Journal of Body Psychotherapy*, 8(1), 19–31.

Johnson, R. (2011). *Knowing in our bones: Exploring the embodied knowledge of somatic educators*. Saarbrucken: Lambert Academic Publishing.

Johnson, R. (2015). Grasping and transforming the embodied experience of oppression. *International Journal of Body Psychotherapy*, 14(1), 80–95.

Jordan, B. (1997). Authoritative knowledge and its construction. In R. E. Davis-Floyd and C. Sargent (Eds.), *Childbirth and authoritative knowledge: Cross-cultural perspectives*, pp. 55–79. Berkeley: University of California Press.

Joy, S., and Kolb, D. A. (2009). Are there cultural differences in learning style? *International Journal of Intercultural Relations*, 33(1), 69–85.

Kira, I. A., Ashby, J. S., Lewandowski, L., Alawneh, A. W. N., Mohanesh, J., and Odenat, L. (2013). Advances in continuous traumatic stress theory: Traumatogenic dynamics and consequences of intergroup conflict: The Palestinian adolescents case. *Psychology*, 4(4), 396.

Kira, I. A., Ashby, J., Lewandowski, L., Smith, I., and Odenat, L. (2012). Gender inequality and its effects in female torture survivors. *Psychology*, 3(4), 352.

Knaster, M. (1996). *Discovering the body's wisdom*. New York: Bantam Books.

Kolb, D. A. (1984). *Experiential learning: Experience as the source of learning and development*. Englewood Cliffs, NJ: Prentice-Hall.

Kolb, D. A., Boyatzis, R. E., and Mainemelis, C. (2001). Experiential learning theory: Previous research and new directions. *Perspectives on Thinking, Learning, and Cognitive Styles*, 1, 227–247.

Kolb, A. Y., and Kolb, D. A. (2012). Experiential learning theory. In N. M. Seel (Ed.), *Encyclopedia of the Sciences of Learning*, pp. 1215–1219. New York: Springer.

Konnikova, M. (2014). No money, no time. *New York Times*, June 13. Retrieved from https://opinionator.blogs.nytimes.com/2014/06/13/no-clocking-out/, accessed March 30, 2017.

Kristy, D. (1996). *George Balanchine: American ballet master*. Minneapolis, MN: Lerner Publications.

Kumashiro, K. (2000). Toward a theory of anti-oppressive education. *Review of Educational Research*, 70(1), 25–53.

Kumashiro, K. (2002). *Troubling education: "Queer" activism and anti-oppressive pedagogy*. New York: Routledge.

Kumashiro, K. K. (2004). Uncertain beginnings: Learning to teach paradoxically. *Theory into Practice*, 43(2), 111–115.

Kumashiro, K., and Ngo, B. (Eds.). (2007). *Six lenses for anti-oppressive education: Partial stories, improbable conversations*. New York: Peter Lang.

Lakoff, G., and Johnson, M. (1999). *Philosophy in the flesh: The embodied mind and its challenge to Western thought*. New York: Basic Books.

Levine, P. A. (1997). *Waking the tiger: Healing trauma: The innate capacity to transform overwhelming experiences* (Vol. 17). Berkeley, CA: North Atlantic Books.

Levine, P. A. (2010). *In an unspoken voice: How the body releases trauma and restores goodness*. Berkeley, CA: North Atlantic Books.

Linden, P. (1994). Somatic literacy: Bringing somatic education into physical education. *Journal of Physical Education, Recreation & Dance*, 65(7), 15–21.

Linden, P. (2015). Transforming the conflictual body. In W. Wagner (Ed.), *AiKiDô*, pp. 159–179. Wiesbaden: Springer.

Lorde, A. (1988). *A burst of light*. London: Sheba Feminist Publishers.

Martín-Baró, I., Aron, A., and Corne, S. (Eds.). (1994). *Writings for a liberation psychology*. Cambridge, MA: Harvard University Press.

Matthews, J. C. (1998). Somatic knowing and education. *Educational Forum*, 62(3), 236–242.

Mauss, M. (1979). *Sociology and psychology: Essays*. London: Routledge.

Mazon, M. (2002). *The Zoot-Suit Riots: The psychology of symbolic annihilation*. Austin: University of Texas Press.

McIntosh, P. (1999). White privilege: Unpacking the invisible knapsack. In E. Lee, D. Menkart, and M. Okazawa-Rey (Eds.), *Beyond heroes and holidays: A practical guide to K-12 anti-racist, multicultural education and staff development*, pp. 79–82. Washington, DC: Network of Educators on the Americas.

McKinley, N. M. (1998). Gender differences in undergraduates' body esteem: The mediating effect of objectified body consciousness and actual/ideal weight discrepancy. *Sex Roles: A Journal of Research*, 39(1), 113–123.

McKinley, N. M., and Hyde, J. S. (1996). The objectified body consciousness scale: Development and validation. *Psychology of Women Quarterly*, 20(2), 181–215.

McRuer, R. (2003). *Desiring disability: Queer theory meets disability studies*. Durham, NC: Duke University Press.

Mehrabian, A. (1971). Nonverbal communication. *Nebraska Symposium on Motivation*, 19, 107–162.

Merleau-Ponty, M. (1945). *Phenomenology of perception*. London: Routledge.

Mezirow, J. (1997). Transformative learning: Theory to practice. *New Directions for Adult and Continuing Education*, 74, 5–12.

Michelson, E. (1998). Re-membering: The return of the body to experiential learning. *Studies in Continuing Education*, 20(2), 217–233.

Mol, S. L., Arntz, A., Metsemakers, J. M., Dinant, G., Vilters-Van Montfort, P. P., and Knottnerus, J. (2005). Symptoms of post-traumatic stress disorder after non-traumatic events: Evidence from an open population study. *British Journal of Psychiatry*, 186(6), 494–499.

Murphy, G., and Murphy, L. B. (1969). *Western psychology*. New York: Basic Books.

Nelson, G., and Prilleltensky, I. (2005). *Community psychology: In pursuit of liberation and well-being*. New York: Palgrave Macmillan.

Nguyen, D. J., and Larson, J. B. (2015). Don't forget about the body: Exploring the curricular possibilities of embodied pedagogy. *Innovative Higher Education*, 40(4), 331–344.

Nijenhuis, E. (2000). Somatoform dissociation: Major symptoms of dissociative disorders. *Trauma and Dissociation*, 1(4), 7–32.

Noland, C. (2009). *Agency and embodiment: Performing gestures/producing culture*. Cambridge, MA: Harvard University Press.

Ogden, P., Minton, K., and Pain, C. (2006). *Trauma and the body: A sensorimotor approach to psychotherapy*. New York: Norton.

O'Sullivan, E. (1999). *Transformative learning: Educational vision for the 21st century*. London: Zed Books.

Parker, R. (2014). Focusing-oriented therapy. In G. Madison (Ed.), *Theory and practice of focusing-oriented psychotherapy: Beyond the talking cure*, pp. 259–272. London: Jessica Kingsley.

Payne, P., Levine, P. A., and Crane-Godreau, M. A. (2015). Somatic experiencing: using interoception and proprioception as core elements of trauma therapy. *Frontiers in*

Psychology, 6. Retrieved from http://journal.frontiersin.org/article/10.3389/fpsyg.2015. 00093/full, accessed March 30, 2017.

Pease, B. (2010). *Undoing privilege: Unearned advantage in a divided world*. London: Zed Books.

Pierce, C. M., Carew, D.Pierce-Gonzales, J. V., and Wills, D. (1978). An experiment in racism: TV commercials. In C. Pierce (Ed.), *Television and education*, pp. 62–88. Beverly Hills, CA: Sage.

Porges, S. W. (2011). *The polyvagal theory: Neurophysiological foundations of emotions, attachment, communication, and self-regulation*. New York: W. W. Norton & Company.

Pregadio, F. (1996). *A short introduction to Chinese alchemy*. Retrieved from www.unive.it/~dsie/pregadio, accessed March 29, 2017.

Price, J., and Shildrick, M. (1999). *Feminist theory and the body*. New York: Routledge.

Privette, G. (1983). Peak experience, peak performance, and flow: A comparative analysis of positive human experiences. *Journal of Personality and Social Psychology*, 45(6), 1361–1368.

Proust, M. (2005). *The Guermantes way: In search of lost time* (Vol. 3) (translated by M. Treharne). New York: Penguin Classics.

Reich, W. (1980). *Character analysis*. New York: Macmillan.

Remland, M. S., Jones, T S , and Brinkman, H. (1995). Interpersonal distance, body orientation, and touch: Effects of culture, gender, and age. *Journal of Social Psychology*, 135(3), 281–297.

Romney, P., Tatum, B., and Jones, J. (1992). Feminist strategies for teaching about oppression: The importance of process. *Women's Studies Quarterly*, 20(1/2), 95–110.

Rothschild, B. (2000). *The body remembers: The psychophysiology of trauma and trauma treatment*. New York: Norton.

Sawicki, J. (1991). *Disciplining Foucault: Feminism, power, and the body*. New York: Routledge.

Scaer, R. (2014). *The body bears the burden: Trauma, dissociation, and disease*. New York: Routledge.

Schmais, C. (1985). Healing processes in group dance therapy. *American Journal of Dance Therapy*, 8(1), 17–36.

Scott, M. J., and Stradling, S. G. (1994). Post-traumatic stress disorder without the trauma. *British Journal of Clinical Psychology*, 33(3), 71–74.

Shapiro, S. B. (1999). *Pedagogy and the politics of the body: A critical praxis* (Vol. 16). Hove: Psychology Press.

Shilling, C. (2012). *The body and social theory*. Thousand Oaks, CA: Sage.

Shor, I. (1992). *Empowering education*. Chicago: University of Chicago Press.

Sokolowski, R. (2000). *Introduction to phenomenology*. Cambridge: Cambridge University Press.

Sommer, R. (1969). *Personal space*. Englewood Cliffs, NJ: Prentice-Hall.

Stolz, S. A. (2015). Embodied learning. *Educational Philosophy and Theory*, 47(5), 474–487.

Sue, D. W. (2010). *Microaggressions in everyday life: Race, gender, and sexual orientation*. Hoboken, NJ: John Wiley & Sons.

Sue, D. W., Capodilupo, C. M., Torino, G. C., Bucceri, J. M., Holder, A. M., Nadal, K. L., and Esquilin, M. (2007). Racial microaggressions in everyday life: Implications for clinical practice. *American Psychologist*, 62(4), 271–286.

Sue, D. W., Jackson, K. F., Rasheed, M. N., and Rasheed, J. M. (2016). *Multicultural social work practice: A competency-based approach to diversity and social justice*. New York: John Wiley & Sons.

Tanaka, S. (2015). Intercorporeality as a theory of social cognition. *Theory and Psychology*, 25(4). Retrieved from http://journals.sagepub.com/doi/pdf/10.1177/0959354315583035, accessed March 29, 2017.

Tsakiris, M. (2017). The multisensory basis of the self: From body to identity to others. *Quarterly Journal of Experimental Psychology*, 70(4), 597–609.

Turner, B. S. (2008). *The body and society: Explorations in social theory.* Thousand Oaks, CA: Sage.

van der Hart, O., van Dijke, A., van Son, M., and Steele, K. (2001). Somatoform dissociation in traumatized World War I combat soldiers: A neglected clinical heritage. *Journal of Trauma and Dissociation*, 1(4), 33–66.

van der Kolk, B. (2015). *The body keeps the score: Brain, mind, and body in the healing of trauma.* New York: Penguin Books.

Vargas, M. F. (1986). *Louder than words: An introduction to nonverbal communication.* Ames: Iowa State Press.

Veblen, T. (1899). *The theory of the leisure class: An economic study in the evolution of institutions.* New York: B. W. Huebsch.

Wagner, A. E., and Shahjahan, R. A. (2015). Centering embodied learning in anti-oppressive pedagogy. *Teaching in Higher Education*, 20(3), 244–254.

Walker, B. (1988). *The women's dictionary of symbols and sacred objects.* New York: Harper & Row.

Waller, G., Hamilton, K., Elliott, P., Lewendon, J., Stopa, L., Waters, A., and Hargreaves, I. (2001). Somatoform dissociation, psychological dissociation, and specific forms of trauma. *Journal of Trauma and Dissociation*, 1(4), 81–98.

Walters, K. L., and Simoni, J. M. (2002). Reconceptualizing Native women's health: An "indigenist" stress-coping model. *American Journal of Public Health*, 92(4), 520–524.

Weiss, G. (1999). *Body images: Embodiment as intercorporeality.* New York: Routledge.

Weiss, G., and Cohen, J. J. (Eds.). (2003). *Thinking the limits of the body.* Albany: State University of New York Press.

Wilcox, H. N. (2009). Embodied ways of knowing, pedagogies, and social justice: Inclusive science and beyond. *NWSA Journal*, 21(2), 104–120.

Young, I. M. (1980). Throwing like a girl: A phenomenology of feminine body comportment motility and spatiality. *Human Studies*, 3(1), 137–156.

Yuasa, Y. (1987). *The body: Toward an Eastern mind–body theory.* Albany: State University of New York Press.

INDEX